The
Sceptical
Gardener

The Sceptical Gardener

The thinking person's guide to good gardening

KEN THOMPSON

The Telegraph

ICON

Published in the UK in 2015
by Icon Books Ltd, Omnibus Business Centre,
39–41 North Road, London N7 9DP
email: info@iconbooks.com
www.iconbooks.com

Sold in the UK, Europe and Asia
by Faber & Faber Ltd, Bloomsbury House,
74–77 Great Russell Street,
London WC1B 3DA or their agents

Distributed in the UK, Europe and Asia
by TBS Ltd, TBS Distribution Centre, Colchester Road,
Frating Green, Colchester CO7 7DW

Distributed in Australia and New Zealand
by Allen & Unwin Pty Ltd,
PO Box 8500, 83 Alexander Street,
Crows Nest, NSW 2065

Distributed in South Africa by
Jonathan Ball, Office B4, The District,
41 Sir Lowry Road, Woodstock 7925

Distributed in India by Penguin Books India,
7th Floor, Infinity Tower – C, DLF Cyber City,
Gurgaon 122002, Haryana

Distributed in Canada by Publishers Group Canada,
76 Stafford Street, Unit 300
Toronto, Ontario M6J 2S1

ISBN: 978-184831-933-2

Typeset in Adobe Caslon by Marie Doherty

Printed and bound in the UK by Clays Ltd, St Ives plc

CONTENTS

ABOUT THE AUTHOR

Ken Thompson was for twenty years a lecturer in the Department of Animal and Plant Sciences at the University of Sheffield. He writes regularly on gardening for the *Daily Telegraph*. His previous book, *Where Do Camels Belong?* (Profile, 2014), was described as 'lively and punchy' by *The Sunday Times*.

INTRODUCTION

For nearly all my adult life I've been a university academic; specifically a plant ecologist. For almost as long I've also been a gardener; the two periods would coincide exactly, were it not that it took me a few years to acquire a garden. But it took me a surprisingly long time to realise that the two strands of my life were really quite closely related. I'm not sure whether there was an actual eureka moment, but if there was it was probably some time in the late 1990s.

As an academic, I spend a lot of time reading papers in scientific journals – in my case, botany and ecology journals. The great majority of these papers are of interest only to a small number of specialists, and a significant proportion are of no interest to anyone, sometimes not even their own authors. But hidden in there are a tiny number of gems that recount findings of interest to gardeners. Or at least, they would be of interest to gardeners if someone bothered to tell them. I looked around and realised that there was no 'someone' doing that, so maybe I should have a go.

But where to start? My eye fell on the magazine *Organic Gardening*, and I emailed its then editor, Gaby Bartai Bevan, who agreed to let me write a monthly column on science for gardeners.

The first column appeared in June 2001, and I wrote one every month for over three years, each inspired by a scientific paper. Gaby paid me £30 per article, which doesn't seem like much now, and frankly didn't seem like much then either. But I didn't mind; the practice was good for me, and demonstrated that there was a market out there for 'gardening science'. It also gave me the confidence to write my first gardening book, *An Ear to the Ground*. This wasn't a collection of published articles, but was in much the same spirit as the *Organic Gardening* column: random bits of gardening science that I found interesting, and that I hoped others would too.

Fast forward to September 2010, when Joanna Fortnam, gardening editor of the *Daily Telegraph*, emailed me to ask if I would be interested in writing a column for her. I said yes, and I've been writing them ever since. Our arrangement, which appears to suit both of us, is marvellously informal – I write something whenever I feel like it, and Joanna prints it whenever she feels like it. In practice many articles are inspired by recent papers in scientific journals, which may be on anything from harlequin ladybirds to the genetics of artichokes and cardoons. Some of the stuff I write about may crop up elsewhere in the media, but much of it doesn't. Several pieces start not with a particular scientific paper, but with a question, such as: is buying bumblebees a good idea, does compost tea do anything, and do wildflowers really like poor soil?

My approach in trying to answer such questions is essentially the one expressed by the motto of the Royal Society, *Nullius in verba* (Latin for 'take nobody's word for it'). That is, I always start by going back to the scientific literature to try to find some actual evidence; I am not (or only rarely anyway) particularly interested in airing my own opinions. Thus, even if I express what looks like an opinion (for example, that forest gardening is unlikely to feed many people beyond those who write books about it, that the panel's advice on *Gardeners' Question Time* isn't always right, or that planting by the moon is – literally – for lunatics), I hope the facts are on my side.

Of course, given a soapbox and an invitation to stand on it, I do occasionally stray quite a long way from the objective, evidence-based ideal. Thus I have, over the years, pondered the relative scarcity of gardeners on *Desert Island Discs*, the waxing and waning of flower names for girls, and why gardeners in literature are always such dummies. I have also expressed my total bafflement at why anyone would bother spraying heather plants bright orange, and why anyone else would be willing to buy plants thus treated. In the spirit of 'all work and no play …' etc., I hope readers will bear with me.

It might have occurred to me eventually, but it was

Joanna who first suggested that the columns should be collected together in a book, so here they are. I have not attempted to update them. Most don't need it, and in any case the updating itself would soon be out of date. In a very few cases, where the article is perhaps a bit of a cliff-hanger, I have added a brief footnote that explains where we are now (in mid-2015). In even fewer cases, a footnote clarifies a topical reference that isn't obvious from the context. Otherwise, the columns are reproduced here in exactly the form in which they were originally written.*

Cerys Hughes at the *Telegraph* undertook the thankless task of selling the idea of a book to publishers, and Duncan Heath was kind enough to recognise that it might fit with Icon Books' aim of publishing 'thought-provoking non-fiction'. So to Cerys and Duncan, my enormous thanks for getting the idea off the ground. To everyone else at Icon, my thanks for seeing the project through to fruition. Special thanks to Gaby Bartai Bevan for giving me my start in writing for gardeners, to Joanna Fortnam for being so consistently (and surprisingly) interested in what I choose to

---

* The great majority of these articles first appeared in the gardening pages of the *Daily Telegraph*, but a few, for one reason or another, did not. In fact, they have never appeared anywhere.

write about, and my wife Pat for putting up with me while I write it. Finally, thanks to you, the reader. If these columns are new to you, I hope you like them, and if you've read them before, I hope you enjoy them all over again. I certainly enjoyed writing them.

GARDEN
WILDLIFE

Birds and house prices

Birds are like people. At least, when it comes to choosing a congenial urban neighbourhood to live in, birds and people share remarkably similar tastes. Ecologists have known for 50 years that many birds like a layered, semi-wooded landscape. That is, they like well-spaced trees, with plenty of smaller trees, shrubs and herbaceous vegetation in the gaps between the big trees; essentially plants at every level from the ankles upwards. The reason is simple – this multi-layered vegetation is best at providing everything birds want out of life: food, nesting sites, protection from predators, and somewhere to perch and sing.

At the same time, students of the human condition have shown that this kind of landscape – wooded but not too wooded, partly open, partly shady, diverse, and above all, *interesting* – appeals to people too. The measure of that appeal is simple: we are prepared to pay more for houses surrounded by that sort of landscape. Not for nothing is the 'leafy suburb' the standard cliché for a desirable place to live, unless you're allergic to gardening, or too poor to afford a gardener. Partly that's because to the human eye it just looks right, but we probably also realise, perhaps only subconsciously, that such landscapes also deliver a range of benefits: reduced noise, wind, dust and air pollution, better rainwater management and less need for air conditioning in summer.

Pleasant as the leafy suburb is, it's quite hard to quantify exactly what it is we like about it. Birds don't worry about such things – they know what they like, and vote with their feet (or wings anyway). This is demonstrated by a recent study in the city of Lubbock, Texas, published in the journal *Urban Ecosystems*, in which a team from Texas Tech University took the logical step of asking: if birds and people like the same kinds of neighbourhoods, can we link birds directly to house prices? They identified and counted the birds in a sample of contrasted urban neighbourhoods, paying particular attention to the less common and more interesting species. That's because some birds, such as European imports like house sparrows and starlings, but also some native birds like the great-tailed grackle, tell you nothing about the quality of a neighbourhood – they're just everywhere. But other birds, such as American robins, blue jays and mockingbirds, are both less common and more discriminating; in a British context, think birds like woodpeckers, nuthatches, siskins and tree sparrows.

They asked a simple question: after we allow for obvious factors like house size and age, total plot size and presence of a garage, can birds help to predict any of the remaining unexplained variation in house prices? Turns out they can, and I'll tell you how much in a moment. But what the analysis also reveals is that while, in theory, the bosky paradise preferred by birds could be provided by public open space or by gardens, or by some combination of the two, in Lubbock (and, I suspect, in many other places too) it's left to gardens to do all the heavy lifting. The researchers checked to see if the presence of a park within half a mile had any effect on either birds or house prices, and found no effect whatsoever. In short, 'green space' is not all the same, and birds are very good at spotting the good stuff. Lubbock's private gardens (or some of them, anyway) provide the varied, multi-layered canopy that birds like, but Lubbock's public parks do not.

So, for those of you who have already concreted over the front garden and are considering paving over the back too, what's the likely damage? Well, the researchers found that on average, the presence of just one more species of less-common bird is linked to a house-price premium of $32,028.*

. . . . ✳ . . . .

Threats to birds

You've probably never heard of the Conservation Evidence Project, and there's no particular reason why you should have. In its own words, it 'summarises evidence from

---

* Or £20,862, at 2015 conversion rates.

the scientific literature about the effects of conservation interventions such as methods of habitat or species management'. Basically it looks at reports of such 'conservation interventions' and asks: did they work? All this is freely available from www.conservationevidence.com, but also, once they have accumulated enough evidence on a particular subject, they produce a synopsis, which 'lists all the possible actions you could take to conserve a given species group or habitat, or to tackle a particular conservation issue', together with how well they worked.

It's early days, and there are just three synopses so far. The first, on bees, tells you for example that artificial nests for solitary bees (essentially an object or container full of holes) work rather well, and that nest boxes for bumblebees usually don't work at all. The second synopsis, on birds, is enormous – 704 pages long. Fortunately, hardly any of this is of any relevance to gardeners, but some of it is, and I have extracted the following nuggets for you:

Bird collisions with windows

Birds can be injured or even killed by flying into windows. Does marking windows with wind chimes, silhouettes of falcons, stickers of eyes or model owls reduce bird collisions? No it doesn't. However, fewer birds fly into windows if they are tinted or largely covered with white cloth. An American study, definitely to be filed under 'interesting but useless', found that fewer birds collided with windows angled at 20° or 40° from the vertical, compared to vertical windows. So if birds flying into your windows is a problem, and you don't want tinted glass, or to have your house rebuilt at 20° to the vertical, it looks like your only option is to keep the curtains closed.

Another American study found that placing bird feeders close to windows reduced the number of collisions. But other studies also found that feeders are used more if they are further from the house, so you pays your money and takes your choice.

Reducing predation by cats

Ultrasonic cat deterrents are devices that emit high-pitched noise above the hearing of humans, but audible to cats. But do they work? A definite 'maybe' here; one study found that an ultrasonic cat deterrent in gardens reduced the number of visits by cats, but another one didn't. There's no evidence, either way, for the effects of ultrasonic cat deterrents on bird populations.

What about fitting something to the cats themselves? Another mixed bag I'm afraid. One trial found that fewer birds (and mammals) were caught by cats fitted with a collar and bell or a collar with a CatAlert™ sonic device. The sonic device worked no better or worse than a bell. But a second trial in the following year found no effect of wearing a CatAlert™ sonic device, or one bell, or even two bells. The successful trial also showed that, clever as cats are, they don't seem able to figure out a way of hunting that makes bells or sonic devices less effective. At least, over the five months of the trial, bells and sonic devices worked as well at the end as they did at the beginning. On the other hand, cats are very good at losing collars, and in fact they managed to lose many of them during the experiments.

An Australian study found that wearing a CatBib™ 'pounce protector' (a neoprene flap that hangs from a collar in front of a cat's front legs, acting either as a visual warning or as a barrier to pouncing) reduced the number of cats catching birds by a massive 81 per cent. Adding a bell had no additional effect. No one asked the cats what they thought of this.

. . . . ❋ . . . .

Homes for birds

More on birds from www.conservationevidence.com.

Not surprisingly, lots of studies across the world (though not all) show that songbirds readily use nest boxes, and most also find that nest boxes increase numbers of birds, or breeding success, or both. So nest boxes are definitely a good thing, but that still leaves plenty of other interesting questions about how to get the best out of them.

For example, is colour of nest boxes important? Yes and no, but mainly no. An old American study compared use of black and green nests by American robins and mourning doves. Robins made more nesting attempts in green nests than in black nests, but there were an equal number of successful attempts in each, so the success rate was higher in black nests. The behaviour of the doves was *exactly* the opposite: more nesting attempts in black nests than green nests, but the same number of successful attempts in each colour, i.e. a higher success rate in green nests. A British study found that blue and great tits preferred green boxes to brown ones. So it looks like every species of bird is different, and since nest boxes are usually a plain neutral colour, there seems no compelling reason not to leave them that way.

On the other hand, orientation probably is important. A British study found that tits avoided nest boxes facing south-west, and that fewer pied flycatcher chicks fledged from south-west facing boxes. So it looks like the official RSPB advice to site nest boxes facing between north and east is right.

Does nest box material matter? Apparently it does. In one American study, warblers strongly preferred empty milk cartons to wooden boxes. In another, eastern bluebirds showed an overwhelming preference for woodcrete (concrete reinforced with wood fibre or sawdust) nest boxes over those made from wood. Meanwhile, a British study found that four species of tits all preferred woodcrete boxes over wood, while an American study also found that tree sparrows preferred woodcrete boxes, and suggested that this may be because they're warmer, allowing the birds to start nesting earlier. So if you're buying a nest box, it looks like the extra expense of a woodcrete box may be worthwhile.

Is it worth cleaning out nest boxes every year? On the one hand, old nest boxes may contain parasites, but on the other, old nesting material may provide a nice comfy base for building a new nest, so it's not obvious whether cleaning them out is a good idea or not.

The evidence from bird preferences is mixed. Five studies found that birds preferred clean nest boxes, one study found birds avoided dirty nest boxes but only if they were really grotty, another study found no preference either way, and two studies found a preference for used nest boxes. In one Canadian study, tree swallows preferred clean, empty boxes, but also liked those where the old material had been left, but sterilised by microwaving. So there's a suggestion that most birds prefer clean nest boxes, but the evidence is not overwhelming. Among the five studies that checked whether nest cleanliness affected nesting success or parasitism levels, none found any effect. On balance, if you currently don't bother to clean out your nest boxes every year, the scientific evidence doesn't offer any very urgent reason to change your behaviour.

Does it help to provide extra nesting material? Two Scottish studies here. In one, blue, great and coal tits strongly preferred empty boxes to those containing a layer of wood shavings. In the other, wood pigeon feathers were put out for songbirds to collect during the nesting season over three years. Not many were used, and when surrounding nests were searched, only 2.8 per cent of the marked feathers turned up in them. The study authors concluded that nest construction is not limited by the availability of nesting material, and therefore providing extra is basically a waste of time.

Finally, tits also strongly prefer nest boxes with round entrance holes to those with a wedge-shaped entrance, but since I never saw a nest box with anything other than a circular entrance, I think that's another observation that goes in the 'interesting but useless' category.

· · · · · · · ❊ · · · · · · · ·

Fear of cats

Some gardeners adore cats, and may also be cat owners, some loathe cats with fanatical intensity, and most of us are somewhere in between. What's not in doubt is that cats kill an awful lot of birds every year in Britain (55 million according to the Mammal Society), plus plenty of other things, from snakes to bats. Surprisingly, however, no one knows if this has any effect on bird numbers. The RSPB, for example, thinks not (for perfectly good reasons), but they don't really know any more than I do. But new research here in Sheffield, published in *Journal of Applied Ecology*, sheds some completely new light on the relationship between birds and cats.

Ecologists have known for a while that predators don't just kill their prey, they also alter their behaviour, and this study looked at the impact of cats on nesting blackbirds. Real cats, of course, are extremely poor at obeying orders, so the researchers used a stuffed tabby, which they placed about 2 metres from a blackbird nest for fifteen minutes before removing it. To check what effect *any* stuffed animal might have, they did the same with a stuffed grey squirrel (a possible nest predator) and a stuffed rabbit (in which blackbirds should have no interest at all).

The effects of the cat were more or less what you would expect. Parent birds responded with loud alarm calls and aggressive behaviour, diving on the cat model and some-times striking it. But in addition, food delivery to the nest was reduced by more than a third, an effect that persisted for at least 90 minutes after the cat was taken away. This kind of reduction is very likely to lead to lower chick growth and survival. Parent blackbirds took much less notice of the stuffed squirrel, and none at all of the rabbit.

The researchers also checked the fate of each nest after a further 24 hours. During that time, nests exposed to squir-rels or rabbits suffered negligible predation, but almost a quarter of nests exposed to the cat were predated, mostly by crows and magpies. The most plausible explanation for this result is that the alarm calls and aggressive behaviour by the parent birds alert predators to the presence of nests that they would otherwise have failed to discover. But it's always possible that responding to the threat of cat preda-tion also reduces the ability of the parent birds to defend against subsequent predation attempts.

Whatever the cause, the results demonstrate that our understanding of predation of songbirds, and of nest fail-ure in general, in places where there are lots of cats (i.e. in towns and cities) is far from complete. In particular, we may sometimes blame crows and magpies for nest preda-tion when the real culprit is already dozing in front of the fire several streets away. It also suggests that well-meaning efforts to reduce the number of birds killed by cats may be misplaced at best, or even counterproductive. Collars fitted with bells or sonic devices are widely recommended, but their effectiveness is suspect, and if they serve to make cats even more obvious to birds, they may simply provoke even more alarm calls and aggressive behaviour, making the problems described above even worse. Research shows that the best predation deterrent is a CatBib™ 'pounce protector', but even this would have no effect on the problem identified here. The only certain solution is to keep cats permanently indoors, which most cats find perfectly acceptable, and is normal practice in the USA. Harder work for cat owners though, so I can't see it catching on.

For what it's worth, it's still hard to argue with the RSPB's verdict that cats don't have much effect on numbers of birds in gardens, if only because – despite cats – there are such large numbers of birds in towns and cities. But the new research suggests that if there were fewer cats, there might be even more.

· · · · · · · · ✳ · · · · · · · ·

Plants for bugs

If you aim to try to keep the wildlife in your garden happy, you probably already know most of what you ought to be doing: grow plenty of flowers that provide pollen and nectar; grow a variety of trees, shrubs and climbers, or a mixed hedge; leave a pile of dead wood in a shady spot; provide water for birds and other animals, or better still, dig a pond; make and use garden compost; feed the birds, go easy on garden chemicals, and don't be too tidy.

Something you're probably less sure about is how far you should endeavour to grow native plants. A few native plant-eating insects are real generalists, able to eat most of what comes their way, but most are more choosy to various extents – some confined to a single plant family, some to a genus, some to a single species. For example, among British butterflies, the grizzled skipper will eat a wide range of species from the rose family, several fritillaries will use any violet, while the white admiral can eat only honeysuckle. Thus it seems only natural that if you want to please as many native insects as possible, you should grow lots of native plants. To some, this is such a self-evident proposition that it scarcely needs testing – in fact 'native is best' has, for many, assumed the status of an axiom of good wildlife gardening practice.

And yet, the evidence stubbornly refuses to conform.

Several major studies have shown no large effect of native plants on the diversity of wildlife in gardens. You may also be uneasily aware that you have grown all the plants mentioned above for years, but the butterflies that are supposed to eat them have so far declined to show up. But for some people (for example Stefan Buczacki in the New Naturalist volume on *Garden Natural History*), the value of growing native plants is so obvious that it simply *must* be true. The difficulty is that, good as gardens already are for wildlife – despite being dominated by alien plants – there's always the possibility that with a few more native plants they could be even better. Personally I don't think it makes much difference how many native plants you grow, but could I put my hand on my heart and say I have the definitive evidence to support that view? No, I could not.

So how do we find out which plants the bugs prefer? The obvious answer is to ask them, or in other words a good, old-fashioned controlled experiment, in which we manipulate plant origin and see what happens. Three cheers then for the Royal Horticultural Society, who are behind the Plants for Bugs project. Replicate plots (each 3 × 3 m) at the RHS's flagship garden at Wisley contain matched sets of plants of three different levels of 'nativeness'. Some plots are planted entirely with British native plants. Other plots take advantage of the fact that all the northern hemisphere's land was stuck together in a single continent, Laurasia, until quite recently, and therefore shares a distinct 'northern temperate flora' that's essentially the same everywhere. Thus all British natives have fairly close relatives in North America and Asia, and often even closer ones in mainland Europe, and it's these close relatives (*Plants for Bugs* calls them 'near natives') that populate a second set of plots. Finally, a third set of plots contains the 'exotics': plants that are as remote as possible, both taxonomically and geographically, from the natives; in practice these hail from the southern hemisphere.

To try to make sure that the degree of 'nativeness' is the only thing that varies between the three sets of plots, plants are carefully matched so that all three in a matching set fill the same 'niche'. For example, each set has a 'tall herbaceous perennial': native *Eupatorium cannabinum* (hemp agrimony), near native *E. maculatum* (Joe Pye weed), and exotic *Verbena bonariensis*. Another plant type is 'slow-growing, small-leaved evergreen shrub': here the native is *Buxus sempervirens* (box), the near native is *Sarcococca confusa* (sweet box) and the exotic is *Pittosporum tenuifolium*. Because differences between any one set of natives, near natives and exotics could be the result of chance, there's more than one set of each, and since location might affect the outcome, the whole experiment is repeated at a second site, also at Wisley but distant from the first site.

The plots were planted up in 2009 and RHS entomologists spent 2010 going over them with a fine-tooth comb to see what the wildlife thinks. They're observing flying insect visitors such as bees and butterflies, trapping slugs, pitfall trapping for ground beetles, woodlice and other ground-living fauna, and sucking leaf-dwelling insects off the foliage with a Vortis suction sampler, essentially an entomological Dyson. All this is working pretty well, and one thing we can say already is that the plots contain plenty of wildlife. For example in 2010 over 2,500 flying insects were observed visiting the plots, including seven species of bumblebee and twelve species of butterfly, while the pitfall traps caught over 8,000 invertebrates consisting of over 130 species, including 30 species of ground beetle and four different woodlice.

The Plants for Bugs project is planned to run throughout 2011 and 2012, so no answers yet I'm afraid,* but for more information including a full plant list, visit www.rhs.org.uk/plants4bugs. Better still, visit Wisley and see the plots for yourself.

· · · · · · · ·✳· · · · · · · · ·

* Four years of data are now available, and the first paper – on pollinators – has now been published, in the *Journal of Applied Ecology*. Briefly, there's no difference between natives and near natives. Exotics are inferior most of the time, but outperform the other groups in late summer. So the best advice is to grow all three, which is what most gardeners do already.

Neonicotinoids and bees

Victorian gardeners were familiar with the alkaloid nicotine as a pesticide, and very good it is too at killing almost anything that moves. Unfortunately that includes people – the nicotine in three or four cigarettes would kill you if you absorbed all of it. As a result nicotine has not been available to amateur gardeners for some time, and approval for professional use was withdrawn in 2009. But in the 1970s chemists developed a new class of insecticides that, although not closely related chemically to nicotine, share the same mode of action and were thus christened neonicotinoids. Like nicotine, neonicotinoids are extremely effective nerve poisons, but unlike nicotine they are really only toxic to insects and are very safe chemicals to use. Neonicotinoids have several other desirable features. Their mode of action is different from other major classes of insecticides such as pyrethroids or organophosphates, which means that even if insects had already evolved resistance to those earlier chemicals, they would have to start from scratch with neonicotinoids. They are also highly systemic, that is, easily and rapidly moved around inside the plant. This means that they can be applied as seed dressings, which are then absorbed by the young plant when the seed germinates, removing the need to spray and more or less eliminating the risk to non-target organisms.

This combination of effectiveness and safety, both to humans and other animals, has resulted in neonicotinoids becoming the fastest-growing type of insecticide in the world, worth €1.5 billion in 2008. Nowadays, 99.8 per cent of maize seed sown in the USA is treated with neonicotinoids (the other 0.2 per cent is organic). Several members of the neonicotinoid family, such as imidacloprid and thiacloprid, are familiar garden insecticides in the UK.* Thiacloprid, for example, is the active ingredient of Bayer Provado.

But no sooner was the crop protection industry congratulating itself on discovering the pesticide equivalent of the philosopher's stone, than problems began to emerge. Because neonicotinoids are so effectively transported around the plant, they can turn up anywhere, including in pollen and nectar. Admittedly, the quantities involved are minute: in lab studies, the single LD_{50} dose (i.e. that kills 50 per cent of dosed individuals) is about one hundred times the amount a honey bee might acquire from a day's nectar-foraging. But a single bee might visit a field of treated oilseed rape every day for several weeks, eventually consuming quite a large dose. Not only that, there's always

---

* In 2013 the European Commission introduced a temporary ban on the use of imidacloprid, clothianidin and thiamethoxam on flowering crops. Research continues to accumulate that neonicotinoids are harmful to bees.

the possibility of so-called 'sublethal' effects, reducing bee lifespan or impairing foraging ability; these subtle effects are much harder to detect than straight mortality.

In recent years, numerous studies have tried to estimate how dangerous neonicotinoids are for bees. Most have used imidacloprid, although there's no reason to believe the other types behave very differently, and most have also used honey bees, largely for practical reasons, although they are not always the most important pollinators, in gardens or elsewhere. So what did these studies find? Well, generally they confirm the original, back-of-the-envelope impression that neonicotinoids don't actually kill bees at the sort of doses they would normally experience. Therefore it also seems unlikely that neonicotinoids are responsible, at least on their own, for so-called Colony Collapse Disorder (CCD), in which whole hives suddenly expire.

The sublethal effects are more interesting. We're talking here about bees' abilities to perform a variety of tasks, including learning and remembering the location of good nectar sources, and ability to return successfully from a remote nectar source. The effects are subtle, but James Cresswell, from the University of Exeter, found that if he analysed the data from all the studies together, a consistent picture emerged. The performance of bees exposed to the sort of dose they might receive from foraging on treated oilseed rape or sunflowers was reduced by anything from

6–16 per cent. That may not sound like much, but it's like waking up with a hangover every day. Except a hangover won't kill you, but a bee that loses its way is a dead bee.

Those results come from studies in which bees were fed realistic doses of neonicotinoids. In contrast, several studies have failed to find much effect on bee colonies under field (or close to field) conditions. The reason seems to be that, as any beekeeper will tell you, honey bee colonies are naturally very variable in the sorts of things measured, such as worker bee lifespan and honey yield, and no study so far has used a sample size big enough to detect the small effects of neonicotinoids with any real confidence.

What about other bees? Bumblebees are extremely abundant in gardens, where they are probably more important pollinators than honey bees, and several studies report effects of neonicotinoids that are very similar to those in honey bees. Bumblebee expert Dave Goulson's team at the University of Stirling have shown that bumblebee colonies exposed to low doses of imidacloprid grew more slowly than control colonies, and crucially produced far fewer queens, potentially reducing the number of colonies in subsequent years. This result is consistent with other studies showing that neonicotinoids make bumblebees lethargic and reluctant to forage.

Extrapolating all this work to the real world is complicated by various factors. On the one hand, especially in gardens, bees are likely to forage on a wide range of plants, only some of which will have been treated with pesticides, thus diluting the effect. The bees most at risk may be those that forage on mass-flowering agricultural crops like rape. On the other hand, the effects of pesticides may be combined with those of other stresses, such as starvation or disease, and the combination may be much worse than either on its own. Since one effect of neonicotinoids is reduced foraging ability, affected bees may often be short of food, which could explain the poor queen output in bumblebees. In one French study on honey bees, a dose of imidacloprid too low to cause any harm on its own had a much worse effect when combined with infection by *Nosema*, a common microsporidian parasite of bees. *Nosema* has been suggested as a cause of CCD, and together with neonicotinoids it looks like as good an explanation as any.

Finally, it's worth noting that in many ways gardens represent the most benign scenario for bees and pesticides, with a great variety of flower sources and probably rather low pesticide use. Out in the agricultural landscape things are far worse, and bees may be exposed to neonicotinoids in surprising ways. At sowing time, contaminated soil dust and talc (used to stop treated seeds sticking together) spread far and wide, coating wildflowers growing nearby and persisting in soil for at least two seasons. To receive a high dose of neonicotinoids, bees don't need to visit a treated crop, or even visit flowers at all for that matter – just being around when the crop is being sown can be fatal.

. . . . ✿ . . . .

Plants for bees

What are the best plants to grow for bees and other pollinators? Observant gardeners already know at least part of the answer to that question. In my own garden, off the top of my head, I guess foxgloves, culinary sage, lavender and an unidentified cotoneaster must be near the top of the list. Nor is there any shortage of advice online. The RHS 'perfect for pollinators' initiative provides a long list of good plants. Yet the RHS list also illustrates the problem; such a list must include plants that are really good and also those that are merely OK, with no obvious way of telling them apart.

To try to introduce a little quantitative rigour to the subject, Professor Francis Ratnieks and his student Mihail Garbuzov at the University of Sussex have come up with a deceptively simple protocol. In the 'snapshot' method, pollinating insects on patches of flowers are counted more or less instantaneously by eye. Measuring the area of each patch means the attractiveness of each plant can then be expressed as the total number of insects per snapshot per square metre. Each single snapshot counts for little on its own, but if you keep doing it, on different plants, in different places and at different times, a picture starts to emerge of the winners and losers in the battle to attract pollinators.

Already, after applying the method to a public garden in Lewes and to experimental plantings on the Sussex campus and at two other sites (the latter reported in the journal *Functional Ecology*), a consistent picture begins to emerge. Probably no bee-friendly gardener will be surprised to learn that marjoram, cardoon, *Echinops*, catmint 'Six Hills Giant', *Agastache foeniculum*, *Echium vulgare* and *Salvia verticillata* are already emerging as winners. Nor that pelargoniums, bedding verbenas, cannas, *Crocosmia* 'Lucifer' and begonias are consistently hopeless. The results also reveal some interesting differences between different pollinators. Borage is very popular with honey bees, although less so with bumblebees, while *Erysimum linifolium* 'Bowles Mauve' is one of the best for butterflies.

But where the method really scores is in revealing the disparity between cultivars of the same plant. Sometimes, of course, these differences are no more than you might have expected. Single dahlias seem to vary in their attractiveness to bees, but the best (including 'Bishop of York' and 'Bishop of Oxford') are outstandingly good. On the other hand, cactus and pompom dahlia varieties are all totally useless (and, although I admit I am exposing my aesthetic prejudices here, pretty ugly too).

Some cultivar differences are more surprising. Lavenders are rightly regarded as excellent plants for bees and butterflies, but are they all the same? No, they're not. Although there is again some variation between cultivars, all varieties of the hybrid *Lavandula* × *intermedia* are better than varieties of *L. angustifolia*. Thus although the RHS website describes old favourite 'Hidcote' (a cultivar of *L. angustifolia*) as 'particularly attractive to bees', it's not as good as the confusingly named 'Hidcote Giant', which is a cultivar of the hybrid. The reason for the consistent difference between the two lavenders is unknown, but the hybrid is sterile and it may be that it carries on producing nectar for longer, rather than diverting its energy into seed production. French lavender (*L. stoechas*), by the way, is about on a par with *L. angustifolia*.

Most gardens are good for pollinators already, but clearly they could be even better. Maybe one day all new cultivars will be routinely assessed for their place on the 'Sussex scale', allowing those of us who want to do our bit for pollinators to select the very best plants with confidence.

· · · · · · · · ❀ · · · · · · · ·

The tree bumblebee

Unless you've been on Mars for the last decade, you will know by now that Britain's pollinating insects are in trouble, and bumblebees are no exception. Of the UK's 24 species, two have become locally extinct in the last century, and a further six are cause for serious concern. The problem, as for much of the rest of our native wildlife, is the spread of intensive farming, and especially the loss of flower-rich grasslands. Bumblebees depend particularly on protein-rich pollen from clovers and other members of the pea family.

And yet, curiously, six species of bumblebees (the 'big six') are doing very well indeed, at least partly because they thrive in gardens. You almost certainly have all six in your garden some of the time, even if not all at once. But the big six don't have our gardens to themselves any more, because Britain has a new bumblebee.

Several bumblebees are found in Europe, but not in Britain, and one that many naturalists always thought 'should' be here is the tree bumblebee, *Bombus hypnorum*. The tree bumblebee is found throughout much of Europe as far north as the Arctic Circle, and it also seems to like gardens, so it's generally become more abundant during the 20th century. So no great surprise among the bee cognoscenti when a specimen was captured on the northern edge of the New Forest in 2001. Note that since bumblebees are social, that is they live in colonies, if you find one bumble-bee, that inevitably means there are plenty more around somewhere.

Since 2001, the tree bumblebee has spread rapidly, with the first records from Wales in 2009. I saw it for the first time in my Sheffield garden in 2010, and in June last year (the peak month for activity of this species) it was by far the commonest bumblebee in my neighbourhood. There seems no reason why it shouldn't eventually colonise the whole country, but it isn't everywhere yet. I looked for it on the south coast of Devon in June last year, and didn't see any.

British bumblebees generally nest in holes in the ground, or on the surface in tussocky grassland, but the tree bumblebee, as its name suggests, nests in holes in trees and is particularly fond of nest boxes provided for birds. These nesting habits are so different from any native bee that there is no reason to expect it to compete with them – it's just an interesting and useful addition to our fauna. Like all bumblebees, *B. hypnorum* is a useful pollinator and completely harmless as long as you leave it alone.

Do you have tree bumblebees in your garden? Four of the big six are variations on the familiar black and yellow-striped theme, one is black all over with a red bottom, and the sixth is tawny all over. Fortunately the tree bumblebee looks nothing like any of them, with a ginger thorax, black abdomen and white tail. If you have trouble remembering that, just imagine a furry mint humbug; no other British bee looks anything like it. If you see one, and especially if you live in Scotland, Ireland or the Isle of Man, which are still waiting for their first records,* the Bees, Wasps & Ants Recording Society (www.bwars.com) would love to hear from you.

I know some people don't like exotic 'invasive' species on principle, but even they can relax. Although our original tree bumblebees presumably came from France or Belgium, as far as we know they got here on their own. No difficulty about that – bumblebees are strong fliers and the Channel is no problem, certainly not with a following wind. So technically that makes the tree bumblebee a native species, because it spread naturally from an area where it was already native, unlike alien species like the harlequin ladybird and the New Zealand flatworm that were introduced into Britain by man. The only surprising thing is that it took so long.

........✳..........

* The first Scottish record was in 2013 and there were numerous records in southern Scotland in 2014.

Urban birds

For many of us, watching the birds that visit our gardens is one of the chief pleasures of gardening. But we tend to take for granted that we see some birds in our gardens but not others. For example, we see plenty of different finches (e.g. chaffinch, goldfinch, greenfinch), but we don't see (or expect to see) any of several species of buntings, even though they're quite closely related to finches.

Why is that? There is certainly no shortage of ideas. A recent European study reckoned it was all about brain size. Birds have been around much longer than people, so towns and cities represent a novel, unusual and rather variable habitat, to which birds with smaller brains might have trouble adapting – basically, maybe urban birds are smarter. The evidence seemed to support that idea; for example, finches do have bigger brains than buntings.

A British study, published in the journal *Global Change Biology*, took a broader view, by looking at both more birds (the European work looked just at songbirds) and at all aspects of their habitats and life history. This study failed to find any evidence that brainier birds are more likely to live in towns. On the other hand, it did find three things that seem to predispose birds to succeed in urban areas. First and most important, urban birds were more likely to be 'generalists' than 'specialists'. To be specific, birds with unusual, specialised habitat requirements are unlikely to succeed in towns; to take an extreme example, red grouse, confined to heather moorland, are extremely unlikely to find anywhere to live in town. Oddly enough, grouse *do* live within the administrative boundary of Sheffield, where I live, but that's because that boundary includes large areas of empty moorland.

Not exactly rocket science, you may think, and I'd be inclined to agree. But the other two things are more interesting. Successful urban birds are more likely to be basically seed eaters, or at least they're less likely to depend entirely on insects for food. Here I think we detect the impact of gardeners. Britons spend £200 million per year on bird food, and most of that is seeds. Studies suggest that at any one time most bird feeders are empty, but if they were all full, that would represent around 2,500 tonnes of bird food. It's hard to provide the same kind of subsidy to insect-eaters, but two things you *can* do are go easy on insecticides, and grow plenty of trees and shrubs.

The third thing is that urban birds are unlikely to nest on or near the ground. The reasons for this are not entirely clear, but there are two possibilities. One is that ground nesters suffer higher levels of predation in towns, especially from cats. The other is that there simply isn't much suitable nesting habitat in towns for ground-nesting birds. There's not much gardeners can do about either (and I don't want to start another argument about cats and birds), but I think there's a message there for planners. At the moment I suspect the needs of ground-nesting birds are not even on the radar of those planning new towns and housing developments, but if they were, maybe we could encourage more ground-nesting birds into our towns and cities.

On the face of it, urban skylarks and meadow pipits may sound bonkers, but it's worth remembering that there's no fundamental reason why more birds shouldn't discover the delights of urban life. Even an archetypal urban dweller like the blackbird 'discovered' gardens only in Victorian times, and it's only in recent decades that the goldfinch has become the common garden bird it is today.

. . . .✻. . . . .

Amphibians in gardens

Apologies for banging on again about the Conservation Evidence Project (www.conservationevidence.com), but they have been having a blitz recently on subjects that are at least of potential interest to gardeners. First birds, now amphibians, and – coming soon – bats.

As usual, the new amphibian synopsis contains much in its 279 pages that is of no interest to gardeners. But some is, including the good news, which will hardly surprise even the least frog-savvy gardener, that amphibians almost always turn up in newly created ponds. Twenty-eight published studies, from Europe, North America and Australia, have looked at amphibian colonisation of new ponds, and *all* of them found that some or all of the ponds were colonised by an assortment of frogs, toads, newts, salamanders, etc.

Of course, little of this work has been done in gardens. The synopsis also reminds you, in case you'd forgotten, that Britain is a long way down the global biodiversity ladder. You have to go no further than Austria to find man-made ponds being colonised by green toads, European tree frogs, marsh frogs, European fire-bellied toads and agile frogs. Even closer to home, a major Danish pond-creation project did wonders for alpine newts and European tree frogs, while nine amphibian species were found in man-made ponds in The Netherlands. Leaving aside the (extremely) debatable pool frog, Britain has only one frog, two toads and three newts. European tree frogs are delightful little animals and I wish – I really wish – we had them in Britain. If it weren't for the English Channel, we probably would by now, but that's the price you pay for living on an island.

So almost any pond is good for amphibians, but are fish? Generally speaking, no. Most studies that have set out to remove fish from ponds have found a positive effect on amphibians, although the water is muddied somewhat by the fact that fish removal isn't all that easy. Netting or electro-fishing often doesn't do a thorough job – in one UK study, even though over 2,000 sticklebacks were removed from one pond, this didn't help great crested newts, probably because the fish were never completely removed, and in any case they were soon back. Chemical control of fish, using the pesticide rotenone, is more effective, but some studies report negative effects on amphibians too. Surprisingly, the best way to control fish is to allow the pond to dry out temporarily. Five studies have tried this and all report improvements in numbers or breeding success of amphibians. Nor does this do other pond life much harm – small ponds naturally dry out, so most pond life has evolved to cope with the occasional drought. But of course the best option is to try to make sure there are no fish in your pond in the first place.

Looking briefly beyond the pond itself, amphibians need damp sheltered places to hide during winter or hot dry summers. Natural England recommend digging a hole about 2 m in length × 1 m wide × 0.5 m deep, then filling it with brick waste and rubble, leaving plenty of spaces. Put tree prunings and leaves on top, cover with a permeable geotextile fabric and spread the excavated soil and turf on top. These work a treat, but are likely to give the neighbours the impression you're trying to hide a dead body. A pile of logs will probably work just as well, especially if covered with turf, and amphibians will often take advantage of unplanned opportunities, such as under sheds or paving slabs.

Gardeners can help, but the biggest threat to amphibians may well be roads. The charity Froglife has over 1,000 volunteer 'toad patrollers', but studies in Germany suggest that the only certain solution is to close minor roads during major migrations. Nor is traffic the only problem; a Scottish study found that 63 per cent of 'gully pots' (the traps beneath roadside drain grilles) contained wildlife, most of it amphibian. The study concluded that gully pots in Perth and Kinross alone trap (and kill) over 47,000 amphibians and mammals every year.

. . . . ✳ . . . .

Bat boxes

It's not difficult to persuade birds to use nest boxes – heck, even I can do it. When it comes to bats, however, we are in different territory altogether. In his 2007 book *Garden Natural History*, Stefan Buczacki devotes one short paragraph to bats, observing effectively that no one knows anything about bats in gardens.

Once again, the Conservation Evidence Project (www.conservationevidence.com) rides to the rescue – up to a point. Their new synopsis of what works – or doesn't – in bat conservation brings together all the evidence they could find, not just on bat boxes but on other conservation measures intended to benefit bats. There's quite a lot on bat boxes, but let me start with two warnings. Not much has changed since Stefan Buczacki's despairing comment: there has still been little scientific research on bat boxes in urban areas, and hardly any in gardens. And second, even in the woodlands where bat boxes are usually tested, reported occupancy is often low. Partly this is because bats are just harder to keep track of than birds. Birds tend to use a single nest box, but bats typically move around a group of roosts, using each for a different purpose – nursery colonies, bachelor pads, night roosts, mating roosts.

But first the good news. In the two studies that looked at trends over time, numbers of bats using boxes increased, so it looks like bat numbers may often be limited by the availability of roosts. There is also surprising unanimity about box location and colour. Boxes in sunny locations were more likely to be occupied than shady ones, and darker-coloured boxes (which absorbed more sunlight and got warmer) were used more than pale-coloured or white boxes. It looks like bats, or temperate ones anyway, like to be warm. Also, perhaps surprisingly, on the few occasions the comparison has been made, boxes on buildings tended to be used more than those on trees.

So, if your bat box is the right colour, and in the right place, does it matter what shape and size it is? Yes it does, but not in any simple way. As the synopsis says, the ten studies that looked at bat box design produced 'varying results'. To try to bring some order to the situation, let's look at the most useful UK study, carried out in a woodland in Buckinghamshire. This compared four woodcrete boxes made by Schwegler (2F, 2FN, 1FS, 1FF), which I won't try to describe – you can find pictures and descriptions on the Schwegler website (www.schwegler-natur.de). They also used an 'Apex' wooden box with a triangular top covered in tough, plastic mesh to allow the bats to grip onto it, and a slit entrance at the bottom, running across the width at the back of the box.

The results were clear: the common brown long-eared bat, perhaps the second most likely bat to turn up in gardens (after the pipistrelle) strongly preferred the 1FS design, which is the largest of the Schwegler boxes, described by them as a 'colony' box, providing 'plenty of space for a large number of individuals to congregate'. Bats are sociable animals, so maybe this isn't too surprising. However, this result is complicated by the fact that, during the bird nesting season, birds rather liked the 1FS box too, and competition from birds at this time forced the bats to use their second favourite, the 2FN box. Very clear is that the wooden Apex box was never used at all. Another UK study also found competition from birds for bat boxes, but showed that providing plenty of bird boxes reduced this competition.

A huge study of over 3,000 boxes by the Vincent Wildlife Trust (www.vwt.org.uk) came to broadly similar conclusions. South-facing boxes were better than north-facing, and woodcrete better than wood. The bats encountered most often by far in their survey were pipistrelles, which is also the bat most likely to turn up in your garden. Conveniently, pipistrelles much preferred the Schwegler 2F 'starter' box, recommended if you're not sure whether or not there are bats in your area. If it's not occupied after a number of years, it's easily converted to a bird box by simply changing the front panel.

So that's my final recommendation: buy a Schwegler 2F box, put it up somewhere sunny and settle down for a potentially long wait. Don't panic if nothing happens at first – when it comes to bat boxes, patience is a great virtue. All the evidence shows that boxes that have been up for a few years are far more likely to be used than recently installed ones. So give it four or five years before abandoning hope, but if there are still no customers, convert your box to a bird box, which is almost guaranteed to work, since birds prefer woodcrete too.

. . . . ✿ . . . .

Birds smell trees

Over hundreds of millions of years, plants have got quite good at finding ways to avoid being eaten by herbivorous insects. Proof of that is that your garden, and the world generally, is basically green, rather than brown. Most plant material, despite sitting there like so many bags of salad, manages to avoid being eaten. Among the many strategies employed by plants to frustrate herbivores, an extremely common one is to have some kind of defence that is switched on only by an actual attack. This defence, usually chemical in nature, may directly affect the insect, for example by inhibiting its feeding, making the plant less digestible, or poisoning the insect. In a variation on this theme, plants activate their defence when they receive a chemical signal from an attacked plant nearby, giving advance warning that an attack is imminent.

Another very common defensive response by plants is to recruit some help, by releasing a chemical signal that attracts the carnivorous enemies of the herbivore. There is an enormous scientific literature on this, virtually all of it concerned with plants attracting other insect predators and parasites. Although birds are prodigious consumers of plant-eating insects, their possible role in all this has largely been ignored, not least because birds are generally assumed not to have much of a sense of smell (which is why bird-pollinated flowers usually lack any scent).

On the other hand, birds certainly consume huge numbers of caterpillars, and there's plenty of evidence to show that plants benefit from this predation. So there should be strong selection pressure for plants to attract insect-eating birds; the question is, do they? To find out, a Dutch team looked at apple trees, one of their main insect herbivores, the winter moth, and one of its main predators, the great tit, in research reported in the journal *Ecology Letters*. Because the peak demand for food by their nestlings matches the main period of activity of winter moth larvae, great tits can get through an awful lot of winter moth caterpillars.

But birds are also extremely sharp-eyed visual predators, so the experiments the team devised to check if they could *smell* infested trees had to be fiendishly clever. They removed the caterpillars themselves so the birds couldn't see them. They also removed the leaves damaged by caterpillars, in case the birds were homing in on leaves with holes in or with visible frass (caterpillar poo). They even carried out a series of experiments in which the birds could either see the trees but not smell them, or couldn't see the trees at all but could only smell them through a cotton screen.

In the end the results were unambiguous: even when deprived of any other possible clues apart from smell, great tits preferred trees infested with winter moth to uninfested trees. In fact, surprisingly, they didn't seem to use visual cues at all; if they could see the trees but not smell them, they showed no preference for infested trees.

What are the chemicals responsible? No one is sure yet, but compared to uninfested trees, infested trees certainly release more of some chemicals and less of others. Infested trees release more α-farnesene, the chemical responsible for the characteristic 'green' smell of apples, and more dodecanal, one of the chemicals that gives citrus peel its characteristic smell.

Whatever the chemicals involved, this is the first time birds have been shown to use smell to find trees attacked by caterpillars – which raises the possibility of breeding plants that are even better at doing this. And it's one more reason, as if you needed one, to welcome great tits into your garden.

. . . . ✳ . . . .

Butterflies and birds

If you're a typical gardener, you're probably rather fond of birds. Together with butterflies, they're probably your favourite wildlife. But what are your favourite birds and butterflies, and why? A team of British and Polish scientists, in a paper in the journal *Oikos*, have tried to answer those questions. Their main aim was to find the best species to inspire people to support conservation initiatives, but the results make interesting reading for gardeners too.

The measure of popularity they used was simply the number of hits obtained when you search Google for different species of birds and butterflies. For butterflies at least, I can see a major flaw in this approach. The most popular butterfly by far, the small white, is 'popular' like vine weevils and slugs are 'popular'; that is, I suspect most people searching for small whites on Google want to know how to kill the little blighters. However, if we ignore that minor hiccup, it turns out that a few simple things determine the birds and butterflies we look up most often on Google.

Size is important, but in opposite directions for birds and butterflies. On average we seem to like small butterflies; indeed our favourite butterfly (excluding the whites) is also our smallest, the small blue. The small copper is very popular too. I've no idea what that means, and it may not mean anything; after all, in absolute terms, all our butterflies are small. On the other hand, we like big birds, maybe because they're both more noticeable and easier to identify; probably only serious twitchers are even aware of all those anonymous – and small – warblers.

Certainly those whose livelihoods depend on catching our attention believe we like big animals of all kinds. An analysis of a decade of the covers of American nature and

41

conservation magazines revealed a preponderance of large carnivores, and especially wolves, bears and big cats. Birds were used less often, but when they were, flamingos, vultures, owls, eagles, hawks and ducks predominated. Relative to their abundance in the real world, songbirds, mice and shrews were almost invisible.

Surprisingly, the *Oikos* study reveals we generally like common birds and butterflies more than rare ones (or at least we spend more time looking for them on Google). I say surprisingly because it is an article of faith among conservationists that rare species are what inspire people to take an interest in conservation of biodiversity. But maybe they're wrong – maybe in fact people are more interested in the common and familiar species they see every day in their parks and gardens. We may be persuaded, briefly at least, to care about condors, but the bird for which we have a real, visceral affection is the robin that alights on our spade whenever we attempt a bit of light gardening.

But the best predictor of bird and butterfly popularity is the number of words in the name; we like short, simple names. Our favourite bird is the blackbird, while the carrion crow, whooper swan and marsh tit all score poorly, and bottom of the heap is the blameless red-necked grebe, whose only crime is to be a three-word bird. For butterflies, if we leave aside the (un)popular whites, we like the small blue, wall brown, wood white and common blue. We don't like the white-letter hairstreak or the silver-washed fritillary, and we *really* don't like the Duke of Burgundy fritillary. Unfortunately the hypothesis that single-word butterflies like the comma and brimstone should be the most popular of all cannot be tested, since both names have common non-butterfly meanings, so a Google search doesn't tell us much.

So maybe – just maybe – the giant panda is such a conservation icon not because it's rare and cuddly, but because it has the good fortune to be called a panda rather than, say, a long-nosed bandicoot or Chinese ferret badger.

········ ❋ ········

Earwigs

I know it's a long time ago, but try to cast your mind back to the excellent 1982 TV adaptation of John Mortimer's play *A Voyage Round My Father*, starring Alan Bates and Laurence Olivier. Mortimer's father was a keen gardener, and one of his chief pleasures seemed to lie in trapping and drowning earwigs, leading to a surreal conversation about whether this would eventually lead to a race of earwigs that could swim. Mortimer's earwigs never did learn to swim, but the play is a glimpse into a lost world when many gardeners seemed to be obsessed by earwigs (the events in the play took place long before 1982). Indeed, at one time no gardening magazine or TV programme seemed to be complete without detailed instructions for trapping earwigs, usually involving a flower pot filled with straw or crumpled paper, upturned on top of a bamboo cane. This advice was generally directed at growers of dahlias, and although earwigs will nibble the edges of dahlia petals, they have rather weak jaws and aren't really capable of doing any serious damage to plants. In fact earwigs are omnivorous and also eat lots of aphids and other small insects, so on balance they're rather to be welcomed.

Nowadays, senseless persecution of earwigs is distinctly out of fashion, and the 2008 RHS book *How to Garden* reflects the modern view by briefly dismissing earwigs as essentially harmless, and indeed positively useful. Nevertheless, the RHS website still can't resist telling you what to spray them with if you feel like it. In my opinion, anyone who feels that earwigs are worth spraying needs to get out more.

How are earwigs doing? Well enough, if my garden is any guide; I came face to face (or nose to pincer) with one recently while sniffing a late rose flower, and several emerged from my so-called 'meadow' when I gave it a strim the other day. In her epic 30-year study of the wildlife in her Leicester garden, Jennifer Owen counted most things, but she didn't bother counting earwigs – like rain or wallpaper, they were just always *there*.

A few earwig facts:

- The urban myth that earwigs will crawl into your ears and lay their eggs there, or eat your brain or whatever, is (of course) false. And despite those fearsome-looking pincers, earwigs are completely harmless to humans.
- The world's largest earwig, which grew up to 80 mm long and was confined to the island of St Helena in the south Atlantic, was recently declared extinct.
- Earwigs have perfectly functional wings, normally folded away under their short, leathery forewings, but they are extremely reluctant fliers.
- Sexing earwigs is easy: male earwigs have strongly curved pincers, while those of females are basically straight, just curving together at the tips.
- Unusually for non-social insects, female earwigs are attentive mothers, guarding their eggs and looking after the young earwigs until they can fend for themselves.
- The common earwig, *Forficula auricularia*, is the only British species that is commonly seen. But the smaller lesser earwig is much commoner than is usually realised, especially in compost heaps. Its Latin name is *Labia minor*, about which the less said the better, except that if you decide to Google it, make sure you spell it right.

NATIVE AND
ALIEN PLANTS –
AND ANIMALS

Plants old and new

If you're planning to attend, or even if you're not, you're quite likely to be aware that the Chelsea Flower Show is 100 years old this year.* You're much less likely to have noticed that the British Ecological Society, the world's oldest ecological society, is also celebrating its centenary. The largest of the BES's centenary celebrations is a whopping conference at ExCeL London in August, but before then, the BES will be putting in its first appearance at Chelsea, in the form of an environment exhibit. The theme will be how Britain's gardens have changed over the last 100 years, with a selection of '1913 plants' and '2013 plants', plus the odd insect.

Some of the 1913 plants, like ferns, are less widely planted now because they have simply become less fashionable or, like the monkey puzzle, people have finally realised just how big they grow, and that sticking them in suburban front lawns was never a very good idea. Others, like Japanese knotweed, have fallen from favour for reasons that are all too obvious. Japanese knotweed, of course, is a nightmare if it escapes into the wild, but it's not much better even if it stays where you put it. If giant hogweed (*Heracleum mantegazzianum*) escapes it can be every bit as troublesome as Japanese knotweed, but Gertrude Jekyll

* This article appeared in May 2013.

was still recommending it as a 'grand plant' as late as the 1920s. Nor was she wrong – fifteen feet tall or more, with umbels the size of cartwheels, it *is* a grand plant, with the emphasis on 'grand'. If you do grow it, and make the mistake of allowing it to set seed, it may escape into the wild, which is a criminal offence. But the taxonomy of the giant hogweeds is a mess, with the current best guess that there are five closely related species at large in the UK, with true *H. mantegazzianum* not the most common. Normally if you are up before the judge for some alleged misdemeanour, the advice is to get yourself a good lawyer, but in this case you want a good taxonomist.

Some 2013 plants just weren't around in 1913. For example dawn redwood (*Metasequoia glyptostroboides*), a beautiful deciduous conifer, was first discovered in China in 1944, but is now widely grown in gardens. Like ginkgo, it is a 'living fossil', known from the fossil record before it was discovered as a living plant.

The hybrid conifer Leyland cypress first arose in 1888, so it *was* around in 1913, but was not commercially available until the 1920s, and didn't really take off until the 1950s. One of Leyland cypress's many claims to fame (or notoriety anyway) is that it was long thought to be just about the only 'bigeneric' hybrid, i.e. hybrid between two different genera, in the conifers. Its parents are Monterey cypress, *Cupressus macrocarpa*, and Nootka or Alaskan cypress. Because the latter was for a long time *Chamaecyparis nootkatensis*, the correct name of Leyland cypress was × *Cupressocyparis leylandii* (that × on the front indicating a hybrid between two genera), and that's still the name you will see most often. Nootka cypress has since been all over the place, but the DNA ultimately reveals it to be a slightly out of the way *Cupressus*, so the hybrid is *not* bigeneric, and its correct name is *Cupressus* × *leylandii* (which at least is easier to spell). If you don't like Leyland cypress, and most of us don't, the good news is that it can't escape into the wild because, like many hybrids, it's sterile.

Another 2013 plant, or group of plants, is the restios, slightly odd southern hemisphere relatives of the grasses. The fashion for restios is recent, but so is the ability to grow them from seed. Only in 1995 was it shown that the seeds of most species will not germinate unless exposed to smoke. The active chemical in smoke was revealed by Australian researchers in 2004 and is now known, for short, as karrikinolide, after an Aboriginal word for smoke. But if you find yourself in conversation with an analytical chemist, you should perhaps know that its 'proper' name is 3-Methyl-2*H*-furo[2,3-*c*]pyran-2-one. That's not going to do you much good in your local pub quiz, but I thought you ought to know.

· · · · · · · ❋ · · · · · · · ·

The rise of the harlequin ladybird

No doubt by now you have made the acquaintance of *Harmonia axyridis* (aka the harlequin ladybird), and if you haven't, you soon will. This Asian ladybird was first recorded in Britain in 2004 and can now be found almost everywhere, although it's still uncommon in Wales and rare in Scotland and the far north of England. But how did it get here, and why is it so successful? The answers to these questions involve a detective story worthy of Sherlock Holmes himself.

Given its native range of China, Japan and the far east of Russia, you could be forgiven for assuming the harlequin came here from Asia. But it didn't – it came from America, but it was far from an overnight success there, or anywhere else for that matter. In fact the harlequin's history is full of surprises. A century ago, its voracious appetite suggested it might make a good biological control agent for a range of insect pests, and attempts to introduce it to the USA for that purpose began as long ago as 1916 and continued on and off throughout the 20th century. Attempts to introduce it to Europe began in 1982, and to South America in 1986. These attempts were uniformly unsuccessful, but then suddenly a thriving population was discovered in Louisiana in 1988, from where it quickly spread to the rest of America and soon most of the rest of the world too. American harlequins turned up in Europe and South America in 2001, South Africa in 2004, and the rest is history – it's already the most widespread ladybird in North America and looks set to become our commonest ladybird, if it isn't already.

Clearly something happened to the harlequin in the South-Eastern USA in the 1980s, and whatever it was, it had much the same effect as being bitten by a radioactive spider had on Peter Parker: the harlequin went into Louisiana a wimp and came out bent on world domination. To understand what happened we have to briefly consider why the harlequin was so unsuccessful for so long, and indeed why most introductions of animals to new habitats fail. Introduced populations always start out small, and a big problem for small populations is inbreeding; because there are few animals around, they end up mating with close relatives, even brothers and sisters. Inbreeding brings together deleterious recessive mutations (which normally lurk undetected in large populations), causing malformation, disease and death.

But there's a twist – geneticists had figured out that small populations *might* go through a process called *purging*, in which the harmful mutations that make inbreeding so dangerous are lost completely. Any population that successfully negotiated this process would emerge not only immune to the detrimental effects of inbreeding, but fitter, faster and better all round. But because the conditions under which it's supposed to occur are so restrictive, purging remained merely a theoretical curiosity – until now. Work by a combined team of American and French biologists has shown beyond any doubt that the Louisiana harlequins were successfully purged of their bad mutations in the 1980s and now grow faster and have more offspring than native Asian harlequins. They're also completely immune to inbreeding – even offspring of matings between siblings show no ill effects at all – which means they can now easily establish from even a tiny starting population. Indeed we are now in the bizarre situation where harlequins could even be invasive back in their *native* range, potentially able to brush aside the native population from which they evolved.

What this means for British gardeners is that the harlequin is going to take over whether you like it or not, and however you feel about that, you should resist the temptation to interfere. If you try to squash any harlequins you see, you may kill native ladybirds by mistake, and in any case the harlequin is now so common and well-established that nothing you do can possibly have any effect on its numbers. As I write this harlequins are out there right now, hoovering up the aphids on my gooseberries, and if they can only develop a taste for gooseberry sawflies, I'll forgive them anything.

* * * ❋ * * *

Native and alien trees

If you are choosing a tree for your garden, several criteria are likely to be important to you. Size, for one. Maybe attractive flowers and autumn colour too. If value for wild-life is important to you, you might consider whether the flowers are useful for pollinators or the fruit for birds. A cherry, a hawthorn or a rowan might appeal to you on both counts.

I suspect you're less likely to consider how many plant-eating insects find your tree's leaves tasty, partly because the question may not have occurred to you, and partly because it's not clear where you would find such information any-way. But all the evidence shows that trees are crucial for garden wildlife, mostly as sources of food for herbivorous insects. These insects are not only an important part of your garden's wildlife in their own right, they are in turn food for many other creatures, especially birds.

So which trees are best for this? And specifically, is nativeness a good guide to wildlife value? Do native trees consistently support more species and individuals of insects than exotic trees? Lots of evidence says they do, but much of this evidence consists of the accumulated lists of insects that have ever been recorded on a particular tree. Which may or may not be a good guide to what you find if you go out and look at actual trees growing in towns and cities.

Simon Leather and colleagues at Imperial College London decided to do just that, and their findings are reported in the journal *Urban Ecosystems*. They looked at bugs (insects with piercing mouthparts), because they're both extremely abundant and a favoured food of insect-eating birds. Specifically Heteroptera (shield bugs and their numerous less conspicuous relatives), Auchenorrhyncha (froghoppers and leafhoppers) and Psylloidea (plant lice) on trees in Bracknell. Some of these trees were in parks or on waste ground, but most were on roundabouts. Bracknell is famous for roundabouts, and some uncharitable folk apparently consider that the entire place *is* simply an overgrown roundabout.

So what did they find? Well, huge variation between different species of trees; so huge in fact that it quite overwhelmed any general distinction between natives and aliens. But if you look at the data, it's clear that the best trees, in terms of numbers of species and individuals of bugs, were natives. The top five trees on both counts were native, with hawthorn, silver birch, ash, oak and goat willow all supporting lots of bugs of many different species. On the other hand, the *worst* trees also tended to be natives; in terms of numbers of species of bugs supported, four of the bottom five were natives. The very worst tree for both numbers and diversity of bugs was holly, and beech and lime weren't much better. So exotic trees weren't exactly bad, they were just kind of middling, with apple and Swedish whitebeam among the best of the bunch.

Which begs all kinds of questions. Not many exotic trees turn up on Bracknell roundabouts, so are the few that do representative of the huge diversity of trees in gardens? We don't know. And although silver birch and hawthorn are outstanding, we don't know how well foreign species of birch or hawthorn would do. The omens are mixed; our native oak is better than American red oak, and field maple is better than sycamore, but there isn't a clear winner between rowan and whitebeam (native and alien *Sorbus* respectively). And we don't know anything about aphids, the commonest bugs of all (as anyone who's parked under a sycamore knows, they're not short of aphids).

The bottom line is that nativeness *alone* is a poor guide to value for native wildlife. In any case, you may not want to grow the best natives, because they're too large (ash, oak) or not very attractive (goat willow). And – perish the thought – growing trees that are magnets for every herbivorous insect in the neighbourhood may not be your highest priority anyway.

* * * ❋ * * *

New Zealand flatworm

While spreading the contents of my compost heap on the garden recently, I unearthed ten New Zealand flatworms, all of them now safely squashed. It's been in the garden for many years, but that's the largest number I've come across at one time. For those of you who have yet to see one of these critters, NZ flatworms are flattened and coated in a sticky mucus. The main colour is dark purple-brown, with a speckled buff/pale yellow margin and lower surface. They spend a lot of their time curled into a spiral, but when fully extended they can be up to 20 cm long. They first turned up in the UK in 1963, in a couple of gardens in Belfast, but very quickly spread to Scotland. They are still much more common in the north of the UK, which fits with their distribution in New Zealand, where they are confined to the cooler and damper parts of the South Island.

Presumably my flatworms arrived the same way they got into the country – with contaminated plants. They have a tendency to hide under objects during the day and their sticky mucus means they can easily be transported stuck to the bottoms of things like plant pots and garden ornaments. They've also been found among the roots of containerised plants, inside plant pots, in manure heaps, and stuck to the bottom of silage bales. They are also extremely fond, as I can testify, of compost heaps. Genetic analysis shows clearly that our flatworms are not the result of a single oversight; they have been introduced from New Zealand on several occasions.

NZ flatworms might have remained just an interesting curiosity if they hadn't turned out to feed exclusively on earthworms. Their slightly macabre strategy is to wrap themselves around their prey, and then kill them by secreting a mucus containing digestive enzymes that immobilises and digests them, before slurping up the resulting liquid. Once people realised that they were here to stay, and what they ate, there was predictable panic about their possible impact on earthworms, and thus on soil structure and drainage, and also on animals that eat earthworms, including hedgehogs, shrews, moles, blackbirds and thrushes. The good news is that early fears of earthworm Armageddon seem not to have been confirmed by events, with some evidence that flatworms and their prey have settled down into an uneasy equilibrium. There are still plenty of worms in my compost heap, so the arrival of the NZ flatworm clearly doesn't spell the end for worms in my garden. There also seem to be an unusual number of fat, well-fed centipedes in the compost heap, which makes me wonder if centipedes eat flatworms. They don't look very appetising (the flatworms that is), but who can tell what's going through the mind of a centipede on the lookout for a snack?

Those of you who live in warmer parts of the country may not have New Zealand flatworms, but you may have an Australian relative, which turned up in the Isles of Scilly and South-West England in the 1980s. It's smaller than the New Zealand variety, orange-brown in colour, and also eats earthworms.

As a postscript, I ran into Clive Edwards, the grandfather of oligochaetology (or whatever the study of earthworms is called), who assured me that he thought the initial hysteria about NZ flatworms had been exaggerated. I'm also reassured that one of the most obvious signs of a serious decline in earthworms would be fewer moles (which eat little else), yet my entirely subjective observations suggest there are currently more moles (or more molehills anyway) than ever.

I'm still going to carry on squashing them though.

. . . . ❋ . . . .

The lynx effect

Most people in Britain live in towns and cities so the chances are that, like me, most of you are urban gardeners. Which, I have to say, has its advantages, one being relative freedom from vertebrate herbivores. So my garden, for example, doesn't look much like my auntie's rural garden, which now contains only plants that rabbits don't like to eat.

Another herbivore causing grief for gardeners who live in or near countryside is deer, with the native roe and Asian muntjac being the most problematic species. There are more deer every year for one simple reason: ultimately deer populations would be limited by food, but before we reach that point, normally by predation. And in Britain we have eliminated all our deer predators.

What would these have been? Biggest, of course, is the brown bear, but we can quickly eliminate bears as a biological control for deer. Bears are omnivores, with plant foods such as nuts, fruit and tubers making up much of their diet, and they eat few deer. In any case, they don't really mix with people.

Wolves, on the other hand, certainly do eat plenty of deer, although they prefer wild boar where they are available. But they also eat livestock, so understandable opposition from farmers is likely to prevent their reintroduction, even though studies demonstrate clearly that the overall economic impact of wolves would be positive.

Which brings us to our third large, extinct predator, and one that receives curiously little attention: the Eurasian lynx. There's a popular misconception that lynx are just overgrown pussy cats, subsisting on mice and rabbits, but this is very far from the truth. The Eurasian lynx is the largest lynx species and, given the option, is something of a deer specialist. Throughout its large range, lynx populations are largest where there are plenty of deer. Like wolves, they do of course take a few sheep, but they are really forest animals, so don't often come into contact with pasture animals. For the same reason, lynx are very unlikely to pose any threat to the vast open spaces of grouse moor. In Switzerland, where lynx have been successfully introduced, the government spends about US$35 million every year on subsidies for sheep farming, but pays out only about US$7,000 (i.e. virtually nothing) in compensation for livestock losses. Lynx are also completely harmless to humans.

Here's something else to consider. Like me, many of you may have noticed that every year, foxes become both more numerous and more uppity. The simple reason is that foxes in Britain find themselves in the very unusual position (for such a small animal) of being our top predator (or at least joint top, with badgers). It's something they're not used to, but they're happy to enjoy it while it lasts. But research shows that in Europe significant numbers of foxes are killed and eaten by lynx.

If we reintroduced the lynx (which, don't forget, has every right to be here, and is absent only because we killed them all), it's very unlikely that most of us would ever see one. What we would notice is fewer deer, and perhaps also fewer foxes, or at least the ones we have might behave a bit less like they own the place. Although, before you get too excited, I should warn you that this effect would probably be limited to Scotland and the north of England; there may be just too many people for the lynx to survive in the south of England.

So, if you're fed up with deer eating your clematis, and the idea of bringing back the lynx appeals to you, what can you do? You could join the Mammal Society (www.mammal.org.uk), who have occasionally shown an interest in the possibility of reintroducing the lynx. Better still, you could donate to the Lynx UK Trust (www.lynxuk.org), a charity dedicated to lynx reintroduction.

. . . . ❋ . . . .

Parakeets

Ring-necked parakeets started out in Africa and India (two different subspecies), but are now well on their way to becoming one of the world's most widespread and successful birds. They are popular as pets, and captive birds have been released (or have escaped) in cities throughout the world, including Paris, Rome, Barcelona and Amsterdam. They escaped in Britain in the 1970s and are now common in Greater London and an area of east Kent centred around

Margate, Broadstairs and Ramsgate. Other smaller populations are scattered around the country, with the total UK population somewhere between 10,000 and 100,000 birds.

So, apart from the noise – they are very noisy birds – should gardeners be worried? Specifically, are ring-necked parakeets likely to do any harm to any of our native birds? The problem, if there is one, is that parakeets nest in second-hand holes made by woodpeckers, or of course the artificial equivalent of woodpecker holes: nest boxes. Parakeets may compete for these nesting holes with garden birds such as great tits, blue tits and starlings, and because they are aggressive and nest early in the year, they could easily pre-empt the available nesting sites. The species identified as being most at risk is the nuthatch, and recent work on the population of parakeets in Brussels strongly suggests a negative impact on nuthatches.

Fortunately the UK has a long-running survey of numbers of breeding birds, run jointly by the British Trust for Ornithology (BTO), the RSPB and the government. A team from the BTO, in a study reported in the journal *Ibis*, has used the survey data to ask if there is any evidence that parakeets reduce the numbers of native hole-nesting birds. The simple answer to this question is that, like the Brussels study, they find a negative association between parakeets and nuthatches, but not with any other native bird.

But the simple answer is not necessarily the right one, because this was not a very clever analysis, and nor was the Belgian one. One could very easily demonstrate a negative association between nuthatches and, say, seagulls or red grouse – that is, where you find one, you tend not to find the other. Not because nuthatches and seagulls (or grouse) compete for anything, or are even likely ever to meet, but simply because they use completely different habitats. The BTO team, of course, were aware of this problem, so they repeated the analysis, only this time they included the effect of habitat. Specifically, *urban* habitat, which parakeets seem to like, and nuthatches don't. The result is that any association between parakeets and nuthatches disappears. That is, parakeets and nuthatches don't overlap a lot, but where they do, there's no evidence that more parakeets means fewer nuthatches.

Another analysis looked not just for any sign of a negative spatial relationship, but also for any evidence that increasing numbers of parakeets has led to a decline in native birds at particular sites. Again they found nothing, or at least nothing involving parakeets. They *did* find evidence that our native hole-nesting birds compete among themselves (maybe for nesting holes, maybe for something else), but it seems that parakeets are not involved in this competition. At least not so far – there is always the possibility that as parakeet numbers continue to increase, and they (perhaps) spread out of their current urban strongholds into more rural areas, they may eventually have a negative impact on our native birds.

In the meantime, there's not much gardeners can do to discourage parakeets from using bird tables or feeders, but if you want to stop them using your nest boxes, the solution is simple: stick to the minimum entrance diameter for blue and great tits of 28 mm. Parakeets need a hole of at least 40 mm.

· · · · · · ·✳· · · · · · · ·

Spanish bluebells

Last week, along with 22 million other people, I received a free copy of the *Sun*'s historic (*sic*) 'This is our England' issue.* Its cover is a rather Peter Blake-esque and very eclectic collage of the English great and good, from Simon Cowell to Nick Clegg. Big Ben is there too, plus a couple of floral nods to Englishness. One of these is a rose, although I suspect most of the genes in the rose depicted are Chinese. The other is a bluebell, which prompts me to say a bit about bluebells in British gardens.

---

* Issued to mark the start of the 2014 football World Cup.

The overwhelming majority of bluebells in gardens are either the Spanish bluebell (*Hyacinthoides hispanica*) or its hybrid with our native bluebell (*H. non-scripta*). A great deal has been written about the insidious threat to the native bluebell posed by its Spanish cousin; it's not that the Spanish bluebell is physically taking over, but that wherever the two meet, the hybrid tends to replace both. The products of crosses between some species are sterile, but this hybrid is emphatically fertile, and is now frequently found in the absence of either parent. The recent rapid spread of the hybrid looks alarming at first sight, but is at least partly an illusion created by better recording; plants that were formerly recorded as Spanish bluebell are now, on closer examination, often found to be the hybrid. For example, RHS Wisley has plenty of bluebells – the hybrid in the garden itself, and the native in the Pinetum and surrounding woodland – but not a single individual of the Spanish species.

How can you tell which one you have? The native bluebell, which you're unlikely to have in your garden, has a nodding, droopy flower spike, while the individual flowers are narrow, parallel-sided, with the tips of the petals turned back on themselves, and the anthers (the male part of the flower, where the pollen is produced) are cream-coloured. The flowers are also deep blue, sometimes looking almost violet. It's also sweetly scented, most obvious when you encounter massed flowering plants on a warm day. The Spanish bluebell is a much more robust plant, with wider leaves and a stout, upright flower spike. The individual flowers are more truly bell-shaped, paler blue, without turned back petals, and the anthers are blue. The hybrid is essentially intermediate, but can look a lot like its Spanish parent, with pale blue anthers. Neither the Spanish bluebell nor the hybrid has much scent.

There's no reason at all why you shouldn't grow Spanish bluebells (or the hybrid) in your garden, although you should be warned that both are highly invasive and will try to take over if you let them. Dead-head thoroughly to stop them seeding; to remove them you will need to dig up the bulbs (which are often annoyingly deep) and beat to a pulp before composting. If you want to grow the native species you will need to use a source you trust, since they are often mislabelled. No one will complain, and you will do no harm, if you collect a *few* seeds from a large native population, although technically you should ask the landowner's permission first. Bluebell seeds should be sown straight away after collection – they will germinate during the following winter. If you already have Spanish bluebells in your garden, attempting to grow the native one is a waste of time – you will simply create more hybrids.

Oh yes, I nearly forgot – which bluebell features in the *Sun*'s celebration of Englishness? I'll leave you to guess, but here's a clue: its identity did nothing to restore my faith in the infallibility of newspaper picture editors.

NOT WORTH
DOING

Painted heathers

As every entomologist knows, a simple way to trap flying insects is to use a yellow water trap, which is just a dish, painted yellow and filled with water. Flying insects are irresistibly drawn to yellow. Wearers of yellow T-shirts often discover the same phenomenon.

Which gave researchers at Rothamsted Research in Hertfordshire an idea. Pollen beetles are a major pest of oilseed rape, which of course has yellow flowers. But what if rape had red flowers, or blue? To find out they started out with a rape cultivar with white flowers, which they grew in compost until they flowered, then washed the compost off their roots and put them in 50 per cent solutions of blue, red or yellow food colouring. The blue and red colours were made by Supercook, while the yellow dye was a 50:50 mixture of Supercook and Langdale yellow food colouring.

The results, published in the journal *Arthropod-Plant Interactions*, were rather fetching. Flowers of the yellow-dyed plants looked a lot like normal rape, while flowers of the red and blue-dyed plants were somewhat streaky, with the dye concentrated mostly along the veins, but still clearly red and blue rather than white. The blue flowers, to my eyes anyway, were really quite attractive. But not to pollen beetles. White and yellow-dyed flowers were infested with pollen beetles as usual, but blue flowers had fewer beetles, and red flowers fewer still. Moreover, it's definitely the flower colour that's having the effect; they checked if all the flowers still smell the same, and they do.

The researchers were mainly checking to see if breeding a red-flowered rape cultivar would be a good way of reducing damage by pollen beetles, and apparently it would. They were not motivated by a desire to transform the white garden at Sissinghurst into a technicolour paradise by the application of E numbers, and it's far from clear that it would work in a garden anyway. They must have got through a lot of food colouring, and I suspect it only worked at all because they plunged bare roots into buckets of the stuff. Heaven knows how much food colouring you would have to apply to soil to get the same effect, or what horrible effects it would have on everything else living in the soil.

Generally, you're stuck with the flower colour that a plant's DNA dictates. Various Yuletide aberrations aside, the only occasion I can recall when living, rooted plants have actually been dyed for horticultural effect was the curious practice of painting heathers. Highland Heathers, a major wholesale nursery business in Argyll in western Scotland, was for a time the largest supplier of heathers in the UK, and one of its more bizarre lines was painted heathers. In fact spray-painted with vegetable-based food dyes, to create a striking array of colours, from emerald green to bright orange and purple. Independent garden centres, large garden centre chains and DIY stores were among their customers.

Personally, I could never quite see the point of painted heathers, nor grasp the motivation of anyone buying them. Highland Heathers ceased trading in 2012, and I haven't seen painted heathers for sale since they went bust. I like to think the idea died with them, but I have a horrible feeling that, like Freddy Krueger, they may not be killed off that easily.*

. . . . ✳ . . . .

Buying bees

One of the joys of living in a modern capitalist economy is that you can buy almost anything. So, of course, you can buy bees. £70 will buy you a cardboard box containing a young colony of the native bumblebee *Bombus terrestris*. For £145 you can have a rather fetching beehive-style wooden box to put it in too.

The question is, however, why would you want to? Well, for a start it will 'reward you with increased pollination of

* There have been numerous sightings of painted heathers since this was written.

fruits, flowers and vegetables'. No particular claim is made that you will be helping to conserve bumblebees, but the blurb notes that 'Bees are probably the most important pollinating insect and their recent decline in numbers has been widely reported', strongly implying that you will be helping to arrest that decline.

A bumblebee nest would, I suggest, have to do a pretty good job of both pollination and conservation to be worth £145. Especially bearing in mind that bumblebee nests are annual affairs, so you would need another £70 next year, although the wooden box can be reused. It's therefore with some sadness that I have to tell you that it will do neither of those things. The conservation argument first. Several British bumblebees are declining, or even extinct, but *Bombus terrestris* is one of the commonest (perhaps *the* commonest) species and is described by the Bees, Wasps & Ants Recording Society as 'not regarded as being scarce or threatened'. I could more or less guarantee to find you several in almost *any* British garden. In other words, it does not need your help.

To believe that a nest will 'reward you with increased pollination of fruits, flowers and vegetables', you would first have to find that pollination is deficient, which is extremely unlikely. Largely owing to the provision of an abundance of different flowers throughout the season by gardeners, private gardens are already close to pollinator heaven, with higher densities of bees and other pollinators than modern intensive farmland. Indeed, recent research has shown that bumblebee nests in farmland survive better if they are within foraging distance of gardens. Another study looked at pollination across a gradient from town to countryside and found better pollination in town; if there is a pollination crisis (and there might well be) it is not taking place in your garden.

Bumblebee nests are also found at higher densities in gardens than in farmland; our current best guess is that there is a bumblebee nest in about half of British gardens. Which means that for half of you, if you bought a nest, you would be buying something you already have. For the rest of you, there is almost certainly a bumblebee nest next door, or at any rate, since bumblebees are strong fliers, scores of nests within easy foraging distance of your garden. The overwhelming majority of these nests are overlooked by gardeners, since unlike honey bee hives they contain only a few hundred workers at most, so there isn't a lot of obvious coming and going. Bumblebees nest in my garden most years, or maybe even every year, because I'm not sure I always notice every nest.

So is there any point in buying bumblebees? To do anything for the bees themselves: no. To improve pollination: no. But the nest is also promoted as 'adding a fascinating new area of interest to be enjoyed by all', and if you like that idea enough to pay £145, then go ahead, although personally I think it's much more fun trying to spot the wild nest you probably have already. Bumblebees are also really good pollinators of some greenhouse crops, in particular tomatoes, because they can do 'buzz pollination' (a technique used by some bees to release pollen that is firmly held by the anthers in some plants), which honey bees can't. So commercial tomato growers routinely put bumblebee nests in their glasshouses to improve pollination. If you grow enough tomatoes to need that service, then the chances are you already know about it, but none of this need concern the average private gardener – just leave the door of your greenhouse open on sunny days and plenty of wild bumblebees will find your tomatoes.

· · · · · · · · ✳ · · · · · · · ·

Grafting

Suppose you want, say, three or four gooseberry bushes. You could always pop down to the garden centre and buy them, but that would be very much a last resort. Much better to find a gooseberry-owning friend or neighbour and ask them to do you a few hardwood cuttings, or just give you the cuttings and let you do it. Failing a friendly gooseberry grower, buy one bush and propagate from that; you will soon have more bushes than you know what to do with.

So far so simple, since gooseberries strike very easily from cuttings and are normally grown on their own roots. But what about plants that are normally grafted? What, for example, about roses? Virtually any rose you buy will be grafted on to a rootstock, so it's easy to get the impression that roses *need* to be grafted, and that the sky will fall in if they are grown on their own roots, but nothing could be further from the truth. Roses are grafted to allow large numbers of plants to be propagated from a small amount of starting material, since every bud can produce a new bush. All that's required is a rootstock, which can be propagated in unlimited numbers from seed or cuttings. In other words, grafting is for the rose grower's convenience, not yours. Roses grow quite happily on their own roots, and for good measure, they are usually more vigorous and longer-lived than grafted roses. Nor will you spend your time digging up unwanted suckers from the rootstock.

Most roses strike easily from hardwood cuttings, so this is certainly the method to try first. Various websites do their best to try to make it look complicated, variously advising digging a trench, adding a layer of sand to the base, and incorporating garden compost into the soil, but none of this is necessary. Just cut some 30 cm lengths of current season's wood in September or October and stick them in the ground, buried about halfway. The only hard thing is remembering to get them the right way up. By the following spring most will have rooted, but take more than you need as an insurance. You can transplant them by June, but they will develop more roots and be less likely to resent being moved if you leave them until the autumn.

But surely some plants need to be grafted? What about apples? Many books and websites simply tell you that apples are propagated by grafting and leave it at that, implying that that's the only sane thing to do. Admittedly, grafting apples does have slightly more point than grafting roses, but only just. Apples are naturally at least moderately vigorous small trees (and some cultivars are very vigorous), so if you want to grow a very restricted form such as a cordon or stepover, you need a dwarfing rootstock such as M27 or M9. But for most purposes, apples can quite easily be grown on their own roots, and like roses, such plants are likely to be less trouble than grafted ones. So, also like roses, if you want to replace an old apple tree, or give one away to a friend, a cutting from your existing tree should be your first option.

The only really important thing to remember about apples on their own roots is that vigour is controlled by the natural vigour of the variety, rather than by the rootstock, so those with small gardens should avoid very vigorous (usually triploid) varieties like Bramley's Seedling. Most other popular varieties, including Cox's Orange Pippin, Worcester and Discovery, are only moderately vigorous. Don't imagine, by the way, that vigour can easily be controlled by pruning. By far the best way to control the vigour of any apple, whether grafted or on its own roots, is to try to ensure a good crop of apples every year, so that should be the only objective of pruning.

．．．．．．．**＊**．．．．．．．．

Planting by the moon

I still recall a letter I read a few years ago in the *National Trust Magazine*. The writer recounted how he sowed his runner beans before the end of April and only two germinated, but when he planted a second batch in May he achieved 90 per cent germination within a fortnight. No great surprise there, you may think; late April/early May is rather a borderline time for the seeds of a subtropical plant like runner beans, and you are taking a chance sowing them before the end of April, even under glass. There is always a risk that an early sowing will just rot, but with every week that passes the weather warms up and your chances of success increase. Did our letter-writer draw this conclusion? No, he did not; a firm believer in planting by the moon, he attributed his success in May to the new moon at that time, which is apparently propitious for runner beans.

You can therefore imagine the sinking feeling with which I read a brief article in a recent issue of the RHS magazine *The Garden*, which attempts to breathe some life into the moribund carcass of moon planting. The main argument is as simple as it is wrong: 'the science is lacking', yet believers 'have a gut feeling that it just might be true', so 'why not?'. Well, the answer to 'why not?' is easy: in 2003, *Which? Gardening* carried out a thorough test of planting by the moon, and showed no difference at all in the yield of calabrese, beetroot or lettuce sown on 'good' days and 'bad' days, using the lunar sowing calendar published annually by Nick Kollerstrom, which is itself based closely on the famous Maria Thun original. Note, by the way, that although we talk loosely about 'planting by the moon', the biodynamic calendar is not strictly about the moon itself, but about its position in front of the twelve constellations of the Zodiac, each of which has an affinity with one of the four elements earth, air, fire and water. So, below-ground crops like carrots need to be sown when the moon is passing through the constellations of Capricorn, Taurus or Virgo – all associated with the earth element.

Just so we understand each other perfectly, am I suggesting you should stop using *any* slightly irrational gardening practice, if it works for you? No I'm not – after all, where would medicine be if we were forbidden from using treatments that seem to work, even if no one has a clue why? What I am suggesting is that you shouldn't waste your time on things that have been convincingly shown *not* to work.

Still, apart from being indicative of a slight softness of the brain, at least planting by the moon is harmless. But here are a few more ideas for you, arranged in approximately declining order of acceptability: ley lines exist; dowsing works; homeopathic medicines differ in their properties from pure water; anthropogenic climate change is a myth; all GM crops are inherently dangerous; the MMR vaccine causes autism; governments are engaged in a conspiracy to hide visits by extra-terrestrial aliens. There's no evidence for any of these, but plenty of people 'have a gut feeling they just might be true', and not all such people are obviously certifiable (although I would take a long detour to avoid anyone who believed *all* of them).

So the next time you are pondering whether the relative positions of objects hundreds of light years away affects the growth of your parsnips, just bear in mind that's the first step down the slippery slope to believing almost anything, for example that Uri Geller really can bend spoons without touching them, or that there actually is a Nigerian out there who would like to make you a present of $5 million. And before you buy someone Kollerstrom's book for Christmas, spend a few moments with Google to check out a few of the other things Kollerstrom believes.

Permaculture

It's no good, I don't get it. Permaculture, that is. And the more I read, the less I get it. According to a recent article in the RHS magazine *The Garden*, permaculture is 'a state of mind or a way of thinking', and involves 'using the energies of the environment, rather than fighting them'. OK, so far so meaningless, but what actually is it? Examples of permaculture mentioned in the *Garden* article include growing ornamentals and edible plants together, composting, collecting rainwater and buffering your greenhouse against extreme temperatures by putting a few large containers of water in it. All well and good, but surely just examples of ordinary good gardening?

On the website of the Permaculture Association, I quickly learn that permaculture will make the world a better place (and me a better person, likely as not), but still nothing about what it is. Back to *The Garden*, which tells me that a primary feature of many permaculture gardens is the 'forest garden', and that I can learn about that from the

Agroforestry Research Trust in Devon. From their website I learn that agroforestry is an agronomic system based on trees, shrubs and perennial plants, which fits with the derivation of 'permaculture' from 'permanent agriculture', i.e. gardening based on not digging things up.

Now we're getting somewhere, but before we go any further, some essential background. At a global scale, the pattern of plant productivity depends on temperature and water, so a world map of productivity reflects that; productive where it's warm and wet, unproductive where it's cold and/or dry. At a smaller scale, soil fertility is crucial: plants grow fast where soils are deep and fertile, but only slowly on shallow, infertile soils. So throughout history, farmers (or anyone trying to grow food) have done two things. First, they've tried to alleviate whatever is limiting local productivity, usually by irrigation or adding fertilisers. But raw productivity itself is little use. If the seedlings I keep pulling up are any guide, if I left my veg plot for a few years it would quickly become an ash wood with an understorey of holly and yew. Certainly very productive in terms of biomass per annum, but nothing particularly edible – at least not by me. Even if could live on ash keys and holly berries, which I doubt, I think the novelty would soon wear off. Which brings me to the second thing farmers strive to do, which is to divert as much productivity as possible into forms we like to eat – essentially roots, tubers, seeds, fruit and leaves.

This boils down to not only growing the right plants, but also constantly selecting the best and tastiest of these.

Back to www.agroforestry.co.uk, which describes a typical forest garden, in terms of the sorts of plants you might grow in all the different layers, from the ground up to the tree canopy. Startlingly, very little of this is actually edible, but maybe I shouldn't be surprised, since the forest garden is supposed to provide 'fruits, nuts, edible leaves, spices, medicinal plant products, poles, fibres for tying, basketry materials, honey, fuelwood, fodder, mulches, game, sap products'. Trouble is, I suspect the average 21st-century gardener has little use for basketry materials, fodder, game or sap products. Nor are some of the other, more useful products exactly abundant; the only nut mentioned is chestnut, which is a non-starter where I live, and although hazel isn't mentioned, it wouldn't matter if it were, since where I live hazelnuts are just an elaborate way of feeding the local squirrels. The only edible leaves mentioned are *Campanula* and lime (*Tilia*), but I suspect that in blind tests, both would come a very distant second to lettuce or spinach. In fact, when you get down to it, forest gardening is apparently all about fruit (24 of the 34 woody plants listed are fruit bushes or trees), so maybe growing your own toilet paper should be a priority as well. Realistic sources of starch are virtually absent, presumably since all the candidates contravene the principles of permaculture (i.e. they actually require cultivation), so somebody, somewhere still needs to be growing potatoes and cereals, unless you want the last chip butty you had to be the last you'll ever have.

How does forest gardening stack up in terms of actually keeping body and soul together? In an entertaining YouTube video, Martin Crawford takes us on a tour of the forest garden at Dartington. At one point he says an acre of forest garden should feed four or five people. Maybe, but he also says if our near relative the orang-utan can live on forest leaves and fruits, then why can't we? Good question, but the highest density of orang-utans ever recorded (in a highly productive rainforest in Sumatra) was seven to ten individuals per square kilometre. You can do the maths, but to save you the trouble I'll do it for you: that's 0.04 orang-utans per acre.

Forest gardens can be beautiful, and great for wildlife, and they can do lots of wonderful things like store carbon, reduce nutrient losses, purify water and regulate local climate, but the orang-utans really are telling us something important about how many human beings could be supported by a world without conventional agriculture.

. . . . ✳ . . . .

Top 10 don'ts

1. Don't waste money on expensive gadgets like compost aerators and tumblers, or on dubious herbal compost activators. The beauty of compost is that nature has been turning green waste into compost for at least 400 million years, and needs almost no encouragement from you to go on doing it. You don't even need a bin, other than for the sake of tidiness. All you really need is patience – given enough of that, anyone will make compost in the end. People who claim not be able to make compost probably can't catch a cold or lose money at the races either.

2. When pruning floribunda and hybrid tea roses, don't waste time carefully cutting every stem to an outward-facing bud. Just cut roses back hard, without worrying about each cut; if you have a lot of roses, you can even use a hedge trimmer. Consider this: when did you last worry about 'outward-facing buds' when trimming a hedge, and has *not* worrying about them ever done your hedge any harm?

3. Don't buy boxes for wildlife to nest and/or hibernate in. Garden centres now sell a range of wildlife homes designed to attract everything from hedgehogs to bees. With the honourable exception of those for birds, the great majority don't work, and even the very few that do aren't worth buying. The only 'wildlife homes' proven to work are those designed to provide nesting holes for solitary bees, but it's simple to make your own for nothing. Drill some holes (4–10 mm diameter) in any old piece of untreated wood and hang somewhere sunny. That's it.

4. Don't just weed out every seedling in your garden on principle.

Among the seedlings and small plants that appear spontaneously in your garden, most will be weeds, but not all. Many of your garden plants are itching to self-seed if you only let them, so take an intelligent interest in young seedlings and keep any that look interesting, at least until you're quite sure what they are.

5. Don't waste money on buying blackcurrant and gooseberry bushes, or on raspberry canes.

Home-grown fruit really is *easy*: plant, pick, eat more or less sums it up. But before you dash off to the garden centre, credit card in hand, take a minute to check if anyone you know already grows what you want. Raspberries sucker so freely that anyone who grows them will already be digging up new canes and throwing them away, so they may as well throw them in your direction. And stick a few currant or gooseberry prunings in the ground in autumn and most will be rooted by the spring.

6. Don't erect a fence until you have considered the rival attractions of planting a hedge.

A hedge will neither rot nor blow down in the next gale. Hedges are cheap, especially if you buy bare-root plants in autumn or winter, make good windbreaks, are permeable to wildlife, last for ever and can provide food and nest sites for birds.

7. Don't waste time and money trying to eliminate moss from your lawn.

Consider why there's moss in your lawn. In a generally damp climate like Britain, moss is a natural component of any short grassland, and can be significantly reduced only by a great deal of work, including (but not limited to) improving drainage and removing any trace of shade. Whatever you do, moss will *always* increase in winter. If you really can't stand moss, have you considered moving to the Mediterranean?

8. When planting a new shrub, ignore any instruction to add organic matter to the soil in the planting hole.

Roots may initially grow well in such a hole, but they often struggle to break out into the surrounding soil. Also the modified soil will tend to dry out in summer, and the hole will tend to fill up with water in winter. Plant a new shrub into unaltered soil, and add the organic matter as a top-dressing after planting.

9. Don't just squash any creepy-crawly on principle.

At any one time, there are probably several thousand species of insects and other invertebrates that call your garden home. Even an experienced naturalist wouldn't know what all of them are, or exactly what they do for a living, and some of the ugliest are among the most useful. Hoverfly larvae are strong candidates for the least attractive animals in the garden, but few creatures are quite as good at hoovering up aphids.

… and finally:

10. Learn from your mistakes.

Don't let a know-it-all like me tell you what to do in the garden, or when to do it, if your experience tells you otherwise.

········•❀•········

Plants worth growing and plants worth buying

If you drive up into the Peak District from where I'm sitting right now, you'll find that long stretches of the road are lined by tussocks of *Deschampsia cespitosa*, tufted hair grass. Once you get there, there are plenty of places where the landscape is dominated by this large, handsome grass. In fact *Deschampsia* is one of Britain's commonest grasses, abundant from sea level almost to the summits of the Cairngorms, and on every soil from acid moorland to alkaline building rubble. So as you can imagine I'm always slightly puzzled when I see folk down the garden centre, loading pots of *Deschampsia* into a trolley at a fiver a time. Put it this way, if I wanted a trillion *Deschampsia* plants, for free, enough pots and compost might be a problem, but the plants themselves would not; a single tussock can easily produce half a million seeds per year, and they germinate easily over a wide range of conditions.

Deschampsia, indeed, comes near the top of my list of a category of plants that you don't hear much about: plants that while certainly worth *growing*, are not worth *buying*. These are plants that even the least observant among us can hardly avoid tripping over while out for a stroll in the country, or even while walking to the shops or taking the kids to school. Among these plants, *Deschampsia* is unusual in that it's a British native; most are garden plants that have escaped from gardens and made themselves at home on road verges, waste ground or walls. Among these escaped aliens, top of the list is surely *Centranthus ruber*, red valerian, a plant that in my experience is now simply everywhere. If you live in the southern half of Britain and cannot find a wall with *Centranthus* on it in half an hour of walking around your neighbourhood, then you really aren't trying. In the west of Britain, much the same applies to *Meconopsis cambrica*, Welsh poppy. That the RHS Plant Finder lists 42 suppliers of *Centranthus* and fourteen suppliers of *Meconopsis* strikes me as nothing more than a testament to human optimism, or gullibility, I'm not quite sure which. If you're actually thinking of paying for either, why not cut out the middleman and simply make a donation to the Distressed Garden Centres' Benevolent Association?

A related category of plants are those that are worth buying, but only once. This is because they either spread vegetatively, or self-seed profusely, or occasionally both. The spreaders are slightly more trouble, in that their aggressive habits can be a problem, and if you want to move them around, you do have the bother of digging bits up and replanting them. The self-seeders are more fun – *they* do the moving around, and often end up in places you would never have thought of planting them, but look surprisingly at home. Top of *this* list is undoubtedly *Alchemilla mollis*, lady's mantle. Believe me, *no one* has only one of these – you either have none or you have a lot.

A few reliable self-seeders are listed below. Self-seeding is very climate-dependent, and some plants that self-seed freely in the south refuse to seed at all in the north. So these are plants that are noted self-seeders at Wisley, and also in Sheffield: *Cyclamen hederifolium*, *Galanthus* spp. (snowdrops), *Helleborus × hybridus*, *Oenothera* spp. (evening primrose), *Sisyrinchium striatum* (pale yellow-eyed grass) and *Stipa tenuissima* (feather grass). Note that if you want pink and white cyclamens, you will need to buy one of each, but once you have you're away – if they're happy, I guarantee you will soon be the owner of your own personal cyclamen farm.

. . . . �֍ . . . .

Plug plants

'Garden-ready organic vegetable plants are on track to being the most popular option for newcomers to the world of organic gardening.' At least that's what major supplier of organic seeds The Organic Gardening Catalogue thinks, according to a press release. Their customers have been getting older, but they reckon that new gardeners, such as busy younger families, are attracted by their new range of baby plants, ready to go straight into the garden to grow on. I don't know how they know that younger gardeners are buying their baby plants, but it sounds reasonable.

The Organic Gardening Catalogue reports that their most popular lines include Cavolo Nero kale, Gardener's Delight tomatoes, Musselburgh leeks, Rowena celeriac and Green Sprouting calabrese. Does this make sense? More specifically, given that not everybody has the time to grow veg from seed, what is worth buying as baby plants, and what isn't?

Like many interesting questions, this one doesn't have a simple answer. You need to mentally juggle the price of seeds, the yield from each seed, the number of plants you want to grow (or have room for), and sometimes how long the seeds live as well.

A packet of Musselburgh, containing 310 seeds, costs £1.78 (plus £1.50 p&p),* while ten baby leeks will set you back £4.25 (plus £5.95 p&p; I'm using Organic Gardening Catalogue prices here for convenience, but other suppliers aren't very different). In other words, ten leeks from seed cost practically nothing (well, all right, about 10p), while leeks grown from young plants will cost you about a pound each. The Organic Gardening Catalogue says 'also lovely pulled and cooked as baby leeks', but honestly, I don't think I could bear to eat baby leeks at that price.

---

* All prices correct as of July 2014.

As it happens, leeks are one of the occasions where seed longevity enters the equation. Seeds of all alliums are notoriously short-lived, so you will actually get 300 leeks from your packet only if you grow 150 per year. Not many of us will do that, which narrows the price gap between seeds and plants from astronomical to merely enormous.

One problem with leeks is the yield per plant: however you look at it, a leek is a leek, which makes paying a pound each look like a bad deal. Five Gardener's Delight tomato plants cost £6.45 (plus p&p), in other words over £2 each. But although a packet of 38 seeds for £1.99 is much cheaper (although ten times more expensive per plant than leeks), each plant will give you a few kilos of tomatoes, so you get more for your money.

Courgette and runner bean plants also look like reasonable value (or less bad value anyway) for the same reason. The problem here is that The Organic Gardening Catalogue would like to sell you five Green Bush courgette plants for £5.35 (plus p&p as usual), and if all five plants do well, you may end up living off courgettes for six weeks in July and August. Buying a packet of seeds for £1.27 at least gives you the option of growing only two or three plants, which may be enough for many people. And courgette seeds are long-lived, so you will eventually see a plant from most of the 25 seeds in your packet. Ten calabrese plants for £4.25 suffers from the same problem; you may not have room for ten plants, and you may not want all that calabrese at one go even if you do.

The bottom line is that buying young plants will always cost you more than growing from seed, sometimes a very great deal more. It's up to you whether the convenience is worth the extra cost, so a lot depends on how you value your time, and whether you're growing veg to save money, or because you enjoy it.

Of course, if you buy your young plants from The Organic Gardening Catalogue, you're helping to fund the work of Garden Organic, the UK's national charity for organic growing. That may appeal to you, but if you were thinking of buying some baby leeks at £1 a time, I have a suggestion: buy your leeks from Tesco, then donate the difference to Garden Organic, which will have the same effect, but save a lot of needless hanging around.

. . . . ❋ . . . .

Compost tea

I hesitated for a long time before writing about compost tea. Mostly because, like all topics that owe more to belief than to evidence, the harder you look, the more confused things get.

At its simplest, compost tea is what you get if you soak a porous bag of compost in a bucket of water for a while. If you do this, some of the nutrients that started out in the compost end up in the water, so you have a liquid fertiliser. No problem there – compost tea works just as well as any other fertiliser. But the claims for compost tea go well beyond that. Compost tea is also, of course, full of microorganisms, and these could be good for your garden and your plants too. Thus compost tea is not simply like the liquid fertiliser made by soaking comfrey or nettles in water for a few weeks – it's more complicated than that.

Which is where the trouble starts. Mainstream compost tea theory is that if you spray it on the leaves of your plants, the microbes compete with disease organisms and keep your plants healthy (or, perhaps, the microbes produce chemicals that inhibit growth of diseases). This is all perfectly plausible. But companies that sell the kit for making compost tea (e.g. www.symbio.co.uk) also maintain that compost tea adds 'beneficial, naturally occurring microbes, bacteria and fungi to your soil', which then 'form part of the soil food web which in turn aids in the natural growth and health of all types of plants'. Also plausible enough, but why compost tea should do this any better than just adding the original compost and its microbes to your soil is not clear, at least to me.

A further complication is that the basic 'bag in a bucket' method produces *anaerobic* compost tea; that is, whatever happens between the compost and the water, it happens largely in the absence of oxygen. If an effort is made to add oxygen, the result is aerated compost tea, which (probably) has rather different properties. The simplest way to do this is frequent, vigorous stirring, but the process can be automated. Symbio's most basic kit includes a bucket, an air pump, pipework and an air diffuser, rather like the ones you see in tropical fish tanks.

So once you've made your compost tea, what does it do? The best piece of research I've seen is a major project completed a few years ago by the UK Horticultural Development Council. They used four different commercially available compost brewers to turn compost (based on green waste, so very similar to home-made compost) into compost tea. They then used the compost tea as a foliar spray and checked its effect on growth, health and presence/absence of pests and diseases in a number of popular garden plants.

What did they find? In a glasshouse study on lavender and choisya, none of the compost teas had any effect on growth or on susceptibility to botrytis (grey mould) or spider mites. The results of a much larger trial, at four different nurseries and using a wider range of plants (the original two, plus *Cordyline*, *Phygelius* and a rose cultivar) were more complicated. Sometimes plants treated with compost tea were taller, sometimes they were shorter, sometimes there was no difference. Sometimes plants treated with compost tea were of higher quality, but often they weren't, and treated choisya plants at one nursery were significantly worse. Generally there were few pests and diseases anyway, but only rarely was there any difference between plants treated with compost tea and those treated with plain water.

In short, the effects of compost teas were 'extremely inconsistent'. These findings agree with other work, much of it in America: occasionally compost teas do something, but mostly they don't. *Which? Gardening* have also trialled compost tea (made using the Symbio kit) on potatoes, and found no effect on blight, or on yield or quality of tubers.

Given that compost tea, whatever else it may be, is certainly a fertiliser, I'm genuinely surprised by how often it seems to do nothing at all. So if you like the idea, go ahead and use compost tea. It's unlikely to do any harm, but almost equally unlikely to do any good.

· · · · · ·�֍· · · · · · ·

Panic in the garden

We all love a good scare story, if the frequency with which they appear in newspapers is any guide. All the better if the actual scary item is more or less harmless, so the frisson of alarm is unaccompanied by any actual danger. Here are three recent examples.

Thousands of species of alien plants are now found in the wild in Britain, the great majority originally grown by gardeners. The overwhelming majority are also quite harmless, but a few do cause problems, and chief among these is the only one most people have actually heard of: Japanese knotweed. Japanese knotweed is feared by gardeners out of all proportion to its capacity to do any real harm. I sometimes talk to gardeners about weeds, and I can more or less guarantee that (a) someone will ask a question about Japanese knotweed, but that (b) no one in the audience will ever have encountered it in their garden.

Not that that prevents headlines claiming that you can't get a mortgage on a property if Japanese knotweed is present, or even that your house might need to be demolished. The latter story just isn't true (the offending knotweed was simply removed), and the Council of Mortgage Lenders says 'There is no blanket policy from lenders which prevents them from lending on properties which have Japanese knotweed', although lenders will probably want to see evidence that it's being dealt with.

Other scare stories suggest that we secretly regret the absence from Britain of any really dangerous wildlife. For example, not long ago newspapers were suddenly full of stories about the dreaded noble false widow spider, *Steatoda nobilis.* The problem, as so often, is in the name. 'False widow' suggests it's more or less the same thing as the black widow, but it's not.

The fact is false widows have been in the UK for over a century, but you're unlikely to see one, and you certainly won't if you live in the north. You're even less likely to be bitten, since false widows are not aggressive. Even if you are, the bite is no worse than a wasp sting, and poses no real threat unless you suffer an allergic reaction or get some dirt in the wound. But so far no allergic reaction has been recorded, and the danger of secondary infection is the same for any minor cut in the garden. The risk of death must be low, since no deaths from false widow bites have ever been recorded in the UK. If you are bitten, it may be some consolation that a close relative, *S. grossa*, is the spider that bit Peter Parker in the first Spider-Man film.

Never mind venomous animals, what about poisonous plants? Several newspapers recently reported the presence of poisonous corncockle in packets of wildflower seeds from Kew's Grow Wild campaign. Since the campaign was promoted on the BBC's *Countryfile*, here was a scare story that offered the irresistible opportunity to kick two venerable institutions at the same time.

In reality corncockle has been available for years in 'cornfield annual' seed mixes from a wide range of suppliers, without anyone (as far as I can tell) being any the worse.

Gardens are full of toxic plants, including (among others): yew, cuckoo pint, spindle, morning glory, rhododendron, castor oil plant, almost any spurge (*Euphorbia*), *Dicentra*, horse chestnut, laburnum, lupin, *Colchicum*, lily of the valley, mistletoe, privet, monkshood, delphinium, hellebore, cherry laurel, foxglove, daphne and any of several ferns. Some of those are *much* more toxic than corncockle, and several have attractive seeds or fruits, making them far more likely to be eaten than corncockle, especially by children. Yet the gardeners that grow them are generally still alive.

Gardens *are* dangerous places, for the unwary, but the things you need to worry about are the usual – and very mundane – suspects, such as lawnmowers, hedgetrimmers, shears, secateurs, bamboo canes, garden forks and hoses. Over 5,000 people are injured every year by flowerpots, but the biggest danger by far is just falling over.

· · · · · · · ·✳· · · · · · · ·

Strange fruit

If you're at all interested in growing your own fruit, the chances are you already have an apple tree, some raspberries and maybe a few gooseberry or blackcurrant bushes – in short, all the fruit you have room for. Which presents growers and retailers of fruit trees and bushes with a problem. Despite fruit breeders coming up with tempting treats like purple raspberries and (allegedly) grit-free pears, I suspect few gardeners are persuaded to grub up their existing fruit and start again. So, faced with the uphill struggle to entice gardeners to part with their hard-earned cash, what's a poor nurseryman supposed to do?

If the catalogue of one popular mail-order nursery that landed on my mat recently is any guide, two strategies are being pursued. Well, three actually, but one can be rapidly discounted as a serious option; few British gardeners are likely to have much success trying to grow subtropical fruits like lemons, oranges and pomegranates outdoors. Citrus exposed to a British winter will just die, and although pomegranates may survive, they won't give you any fruit.

A more realistic option is to inveigle us into growing native trees and shrubs that we perhaps wouldn't consider growing for their fruit, a reluctance that is, in my opinion, entirely justified. There's no earthly reason to try to grow juniper berries unless you are bent on making your own gin, although that would at least give you an excuse to grow blackthorn, whose fruits are of no use other than for making sloe gin. Dewberries are essentially just blackberries that are lower-yielding and harder to pick, so why bother? The best my catalogue can say about the fruits of the cowberry (now rebranded as lingonberry, perhaps in deference to our burgeoning love affair with IKEA and Nordic crime fiction) is that they are 'tart', and in *Food for Free*, Richard Mabey says they are 'scarcely edible', at least when raw. I couldn't agree more. As for crowberry (*Empetrum*), Mabey describes them as 'poor eating'; I've tried them and that opinion strikes me as really quite generous – you have been warned. A related plant that *is* worth eating, but certainly not worth growing, is bilberry. If you have any nearby moorland, take a walk and pick some from the wild, thus profitably combining fresh air, exercise *and* delicious fruit. If you don't live in the right part of the country, but still have a hankering after *Vaccinium*, stick to blueberries.

The second option is to plunder the vast store of exotic temperate fruits you've never even heard of, with the vast rose family often the first port of call. The Rosaceae is full of stuff you eat already, for example apples, pears, plums, raspberries, peaches and strawberries, plus some you've always meant to try but somehow never got round to, like medlars and loquats, so it's only natural that nurserymen would try to interest us in all those we never even knew existed. *Rubus* is a good place to start, with hundreds of species, around 60 of them in cultivation, and all producing vaguely raspberry- or blackberry-like fruits. One that has long been grown for its fruits, although curiously only rarely in Britain, is Japanese wineberry (*Rubus phoenicolasius*), with fruits that look like a raspberry, but on a plant that looks more like a blackberry. Highly recommended by both gardening writer Ursula Buchan and fruit legend Ken Muir, this is definitely one to try if you have the space.

On the other hand, it's not safe to assume that any old *Rubus* is worth growing for its fruit. My catalogue offers the balloon berry (*Rubus illecebrosus*), also from Japan. With its short, creeping growth habit, this species is sometimes called the strawberry raspberry. Sounds good, doesn't it, and yet no one seems really enthusiastic; the catalogue describes the fruits as 'fairly bland, much better cooked', and one website, perhaps slightly more truthfully, says 'can be cooked to make them palatable'. In any case, *R. illecebrosus* is one of several species that have been used by breeders to improve the wild raspberry, *R. idaeus*, so if you grow a modern raspberry variety, you are already getting the benefit of the balloon berry's 'best' genes, without the bother of actually growing it.

Most woody Rosaceae have fruit of some sort. Many of us already grow *Amelanchier* (juneberry) and *Aronia* (chokeberry) as ornamentals, so why not eat the fruit as well? (We could often do more of this – fuchsia crumble, anyone?) *Amelanchier alnifolia* is widely grown and eaten in America, where it's known as saskatoon. I haven't tried it, but plenty of people think it's delicious, and in any case the flowers are as pretty as in the more widely grown ornamental species, so what have you got to lose? *Aronia* I'm less sure about;

even my catalogue says 'too tart and sharp to eat fresh', while the *Journal of the American Pomological Society* damns this 'semi-edible' fruit with very faint praise: 'the somewhat unpleasant taste of the raw fruit may limit its use to blended juices, liqueurs, and medicinal products'. I think it's that 'medicinal products' that kills it for me.

Don't let me put you off growing any of these plants if you enjoy an adventure, but my advice is to stick to plants that actually have a history as food, and ideally taste before you buy; after all, why go for something untried if you don't *already* grow black mulberry, my candidate for the most delicious thing you can grow outside the tropics? The only downside to a mulberry is that it will – eventually – make a moderately large tree, so for something smaller (and also new, but reassuringly familiar), try a plum–apricot hybrid, sometimes called a plumcot (if about 50:50) or a pluot (if more plum than apricot). And you can try them first, from Waitrose!

Must have   black mulberry
autumn raspberries (much easier to grow
than summer variety)
damson (the ultimate fruit for jam)
greengage (rich, intense aromatic fruit)

Worth trying	plumcot
	Japanese wineberry
	hybrid berries, e.g. loganberry (tasty but needs a lot of space)
	kiwi fruit (new self-fertile varieties)
	quince (the true quince, not *Chaenomeles*)
	fig, peach, nectarine (only in warm gardens)
	goji berry (grow them if you like the flavour, but you're still not going to live for ever)
Don't bother	blackthorn
	juniper
	bilberry (pick from the wild)
	cowberry
	crowberry
	blackberry (pick from the wild)
	dewberry
	cherry (unless you like feeding the birds)
	olive
	loquat (hardy but rarely fruits in Britain)
	pawpaw (hardy but doesn't fruit well in British summers, and an acquired taste anyway)

NAMES OF
PLANTS –
AND PEOPLE

Flower names for girls

Every summer, publication of the top baby names for the previous year provokes a flurry of newspaper articles. But for the keen gardener, perhaps the most fascinating aspect of these lists lies in the astonishing fall and rise in the popularity of plants and flowers as names for baby girls. The trend can be followed on the website of the Office for National Statistics, which lists the top 100 girls' names for every tenth year from 1904 to 1994, and then for every year from 1996 onwards.

The Edwardian era was the heyday of flower names for girls, with Ivy, Violet, Lily, Rose, Daisy, May, Iris and Olive all in the top 100 in 1904 and 1914, although none made the top ten – Mary was top in both years. Thereafter it was downhill all the way for most of the century, with the nadir being reached in 1974, when the top 100 contained just a single plant name: Heather. I don't have information for every year, but I wouldn't be surprised if sometime in the 1960s or 70s there was at least one year when there were no flower names at all in the top 100 (there were only two in 1964).

Curiously, however, after 1974 things began to look up, with three flower names in the top 100 in 1984, eight in 1994 and nine in 1996. In fact the last six years have achieved something the Edwardians never managed, which is a flower name in the top ten, indeed the same one in all those years: Lily. If we were to count Lilly as a variation on Lily, the combined total would easily have come top in 2011, by a wide margin. Not far behind Lily is another Edwardian favourite, Daisy; both re-entered the lists after a long absence in 1994 and have risen in popularity ever since, Daisy reaching its highest rank (fifteenth) in 2010. Rose (and its variant Rosie) has also seen a major recovery in recent years.

But the news on the other Edwardian favourites is grim: no renaissance for Ivy, Violet or Olive, last seen in 1934, or Iris, not seen since 1944. It's hard to say why. Maybe Olive never recovered from Popeye's fickle and bad-tempered squeeze, Olive Oyl, and perhaps successive generations have been scarred by Just William's nemesis Violet Elizabeth Bott ('I'll thcream and thcream till I'm thick'), or still have night-mares about Ena Sharples' (played by Violet Carson) hair net and milk stout in *Coronation Street*. The decline of Olive is particularly surprising when you consider that a minor variation, Olivia, has been extraordinarily popular since its first appearance in 1994, coming top in 2008, 2009 and 2010.

But recent top 100s are peppered with flower names: ten in 2011. So what are they? Poppy, Jasmine and Holly (or Hollie) are the other popular names in recent years. All three first appeared in the mid-90s and have been popular ever since, especially Holly, which reached the highest rank for a flower name before the meteoric rise of Lily, reaching twelfth in 2002. Willow is one to watch too, in at 75 for the first time in 2011.

All these are, of course, English names. Latin plant names are rare in the top 100, with only three having ever made an appearance (five if we include Iris and Daphne, which both double as Latin and English names, and last appeared in 1944). Veronica (speedwell) crept in at 83 in 1934, rose to 52 in 1944 and fell to 98 in 1954, corresponding perfectly to the career of Hollywood *femme fatale* Veronica Lake. Melissa (lemon balm) arrived in 1984, reached its highest rank (41) in 1994, and then slowly declined in popularity and was last seen in 2004. Phoebe (a tree in the laurel family) appeared suddenly in 1996 and has been popular ever since, showing (I guess) the continuing grip on the popular imagination of *Friends*.

Despite the occasional celebrity endorsement (e.g. Prunella, Nigella), no other Latin name appears in any top 100, suggesting (to me anyway) that Latin names are rather underemployed as girls' names. Is there anyone out there called Ramonda or Azara, and if not, why not? Finally, do flowers have any future as names for boys? I don't think so – after all, Narcissus was a bloke, and look what happened to him.

. . . . ❋ . . . .

Plant names – common or Latin?

Speaking as a botanist, and thus signed up by default to Linnaean binomial nomenclature, I'm probably the last person to complain about common names of plants. But I did have a bit of an epiphany the other day, while reading a new account of the native and naturalised plants of the Royal Horticultural Society's garden at Wisley. Listed there is *Cyclamen hederifolium*, which seems to have made itself just as much at home at Wisley as it has in my garden. What struck me, however, was the common name of *Cyclamen hederifolium*: sowbread. Sowbread? In fact I've known for a long time, in a rather abstract way, that sowbread is the common name for cyclamen. But what hadn't quite dawned on me before is that I can't recall *anyone* ever using the name. Among all the botanists and gardeners of my acquaintance, cyclamens are just, well, cyclamens.

Which set me musing on the question: when is a common name not a common name? The Wisley list is clearly predicated on the assumption that every plant has a common name, whether it likes it or not, but in fact common names occupy a complete spectrum, from names that are genuinely in common use at one extreme to practically non-existent at the other, taking in extremely obscure along the way. At the common end of the spectrum are names like snowdrop, oak, pine and willow, which are universally understood and which even botanists tend to prefer to their Latin equivalents.

In the middle ground are plants where Latin and common names exist in a kind of uneasy equilibrium. Think *Geranium*/cranesbill, *Aquilegia*/columbine, *Nigella*/love-in-a-mist, *Verbascum*/mullein and *Lonicera*/honeysuckle. Also in here somewhere are all those uncomplicated plants where the Latin name *is* the common name: rhododendron, iris, crocus, wisteria, camellia, penstemon and many, many more. Unless some bright spark has dreamed up a 'common' name for rhododendrons while I wasn't looking (and if anyone *has*, I really don't want to know).

Sowbread is close to the obscure extreme, but I think we can do even better than that. Also according to the Wisley list, hostas are 'August lilies', a name that fails any test of 'commonness' you care to devise. Google 'August lily' and you get about 31,000 hits, but many of those aren't even plants (it appears to be a popular name for florists, and there also seem to be quite a few people called August Lily), while most of those that are seem to be *Lycoris squamigera*, a different plant altogether. Google 'hosta', on the other hand, and you get over 8 million hits, which I think tells you all you need to know about the popularity of 'August lily'.

Then there are those annoying plants that have become fashionable only recently, and where anyone and everyone still feels entitled to their own opinion of what the common name should be. Take the elegant bulb *Nectaroscordum siculum*. 'Honey garlic' in the Wisley list, but otherwise variously ornamental onion, Sicilian honey garlic, Mediterranean bells, Bulgarian allium, honey lily, Bulgarian onion, and so on.

So here are Thompson's rules for common names of garden plants:

1. If you have to look up a common name before you can use it, don't. If you didn't know the name, why do you expect anyone else to have heard of it?

2. If the first three suppliers you check on the internet don't mention a common name, the plant you're looking for doesn't have one.

3. If the first three suppliers you check *do* use a common name, but all three are different, see previous point.

4. If you want to be sure you come away with the plant you want, stick to Latin. If you know enough to realise that what you're really hankering after is *Echium pininana* × *wildpretii*, why would you waste everyone's time by asking for a hybrid tree echium?

. . . . ❋ . . . .

DNA and plant names

The relief of just being able to attach a name to a plant is probably enough for most gardeners, but botanists, and many keen gardeners too, are interested in how plants fit together into a classification. You can classify plants in any way you like, and gardeners often do; growth form, flower colour and flowering time are popular, as is habitat preference ('plants for dry shade' etc.). But a good botanical classification should reflect evolutionary history, or *phylogeny* in the jargon: if plants are close together in the classification, that's because they are closely related. Different buttercups or oaks are similar because they diverged relatively recently (in geological terms) from a common buttercup-like or oak-like ancestor, and the whole classification is essentially a giant family tree.

Once upon a time plants were classified on the basis of their appearance, on the perfectly reasonable assumption that plants that looked similar must be closely related. But for the last 50 years we've known that evolution proceeds by the accumulation of tiny mutations in DNA, so that the similarity of the DNA of two species is a perfect representation of how closely related they are. Thus, as we are frequently informed, humans and chimpanzees are closely related, and in fact share 99 per cent of their DNA. Increasingly, we are using DNA itself to classify plants and animals, and it's reassuring to find that modern classifications based directly on DNA are generally similar, and in fact often identical, to older classifications based on outward appearance. But not always, resulting in quite a bit of recent rearrangement of the taxonomic furniture.

Sometimes the changes involved are hard to take, however much you know they must be right. Few among you, I imagine, will have looked at sycamore and horse chestnut and thought to yourself how similar they are. In fact, given the profound differences in their leaves, flowers and seeds, the possibility that they might be related probably never crossed your mind. But not only does the DNA say they are, it says the families to which each gave its name (the Aceraceae, or maple family, and the Hippocastanaceae, or horse chestnut family) don't exist, and that both trees belong in the mainly tropical Sapindaceae, chiefly notable for the fruits lychee and rambutan.

Other major changes don't exactly make life simpler, and can involve altering the habits of a lifetime. The DNA evidence has revealed the Scrophulariaceae, once one of the largest families in the British flora, to be a mish-mash of only distantly related plants. The result is that my lifelong habit of referring to the Scrophulariaceae as 'the foxglove family' will have to stop, since foxglove isn't even *in* the new, emaciated Scrophulariaceae. On the other hand, buddleia is, and *its* family, the Buddlejaceae, ceases to exist.

More often the rearrangement is at lower levels, and on occasion the changes are quite satisfying, uniting plants that you suspected were the same anyway. Within the mallow family (Malvaceae), those of you who always thought that mallows (*Malva* species), marsh-mallows (*Althaea* species) and lavateras looked pretty similar can award yourselves a gold star, because the DNA is on your side; these three genera cannot be separated in any way that makes sense, and all belong in an enlarged *Malva*. Thus the very beautiful and deservedly popular *Lavatera trimestris* becomes *Malva trimestris*.

Sometimes, uniting (or reuniting) plants formerly thought to be distinct isn't so welcome. Those of you who like to grow the charming spring bulb *Chionodoxa luciliae* will find that you are now growing *Scilla luciliae*, and your *Lychnis coronaria* needs a new label too; it's now *Silene coronaria*. Another change that will take some getting used to is the complete disappearance of the genus *Hebe*, subsumed into *Veronica*. It turns out that the character used to separate these genera (essentially woody = *Hebe*, herbaceous = *Veronica*) isn't worth a damn, and simply doesn't reflect genetic reality: hebes and veronicas are a complete mixture.

The joy of all previous classifications was that they were essentially a reflection of someone's opinion of what was important and what wasn't, and that could change over time. Thus they were a bit like buses; if you didn't like the current one, a different one would be along soon. For example, it's ironic that hebes were long considered to be veronicas (that's how Gertrude Jekyll knew them), and gardeners took a long time to be persuaded that they were different. But the good news – or bad news, depending on your point of view – is that the latest classification, apart from the odd bit of tidying up, is here to stay – DNA doesn't just *reflect* relationships between plants, it *is* that relationship. The DNA revolution may be messing up some bits of the plant kingdom that we'd prefer left alone, but at least it will never happen again. So, with apologies to the many dedicated members of the Hebe Society, hebes are gone, and they aren't coming back.

. . . . ✳ . . . .

It's Hesperantha, *not* Schizostylis

It's hardly fair, is it? You spend years learning how to spell *Schizostylis*, then one day you wake up and find you're growing *Hesperantha* instead. The change of name is a nice illustration of how long it takes gardening to catch up with the boffins, who realised *Schizostylis* doesn't deserve a genus of its own as long ago as 1996. Nevertheless Googling *Schizostylis* still produces twice as many hits as *Hesperantha*.

How did *Schizostylis* come to be seen as distinct from *Hesperantha* in the first place? In almost every detail, *Schizostylis* is identical to *Hesperantha*. Take a good look at your *Schizostylis*, and then try Googling a picture of, say, *H. woodii* or *H. grandiflora* and see if you can tell the difference. The only real distinction is that all other species of *Hesperantha* grow from a corm, while *Schizostylis* has a short rhizome. But this seems to be a result of a simple change of habitat. Corms are characteristic of plants of dry habitats, which is where *Hesperantha* species generally grow, but *Schizostylis* seems to be simply a *Hesperantha* that has moved into much wetter places such as riverbanks and edges of marshes, habitats where rhizomes are more common. The only other difference is that most *Hesperantha* species have pink flowers, while *Schizostylis* is bright red, but since forms of *Schizostylis* with pink flowers are found in cultivation and in the wild, that doesn't seem to count for much. The final nail in the coffin of *Schizostylis* is the DNA data, which confirms that the two genera cannot be separated.

One positive outcome of the confusion may be that gardeners take a bit more notice of *Hesperantha*; although there are 79 species, they are hardly grown in British gardens, with only a handful available according to the RHS Plant Finder. Alternatively, you could use the genus as an excuse for a trip to the Drakensberg mountains in South Africa, which is where most of them come from. Most species, unlike *Schizostylis*, flower in the spring and have attractive pink (but sometimes yellow, purple or white) flowers. They are also likely to prove a bit more well-behaved than *Schizostylis*, which many gardeners will know can be alarmingly invasive in a damp spot. Another problem with *Schizostylis* is that it is sold under a bewildering and ever-changing range of cultivar names, many of which are exactly the same plant, while plants sold under the same name sometimes turn out to be different. In my experience shades of pink are particularly hard to pin down, and the best advice to the would-be purchaser is to see the plant in flower before you buy.

It's worth noting that the Latin name is not the only source of confusion. Political correctness catches up with us all in the end, and *Hesperantha coccinea* (as we must now call *Schizostylis*) is no exception. It's always been known, to me and gardeners of my acquaintance anyway, as kaffir lily. But kaffir is an offensive term for black South Africans, about on a par with 'n*****'. I suspect no one outside South Africa is likely to consider 'kaffir lily' a racial slur, but nevertheless I sense a campaign is afoot to find something more inoffensive. Crimson flag lily, Cape lily and river lily, or scarlet river lily, all appear to be in circulation, but if you decide to use any of them, don't blame me if no one has a clue what you're talking about.

⚹

Hyphens and capitals

Correspondence has been rumbling on in the pages of *BSBI News*, the 'popular' publication for members of the Botanical Society of the British Isles, about how English names of plants should be written. Specifically about the use of hyphens and initial capital letters.

Believe me, life is too short to even attempt to summarise the arguments for why (a) there are too many hyphens in plant names, and (b) they are in the wrong place. Granted, hyphens are illogical (in the official Wildflower Society list, why wild-oat for *Avena fatua* but water fern for *Azolla*?), but if we wanted logic, we'd all be speaking Esperanto. There is no more doomed enterprise than trying to rationalise something that neither needs nor wants to be rationalised. Whatever I or anyone else says, hyphens will continue to appear where centuries of custom and practice dictate, and there's an end to the matter.

Initial capital letters for plant (and animal) names are more interesting, if only because you may be mystified why anyone would consider them desirable in the first place. And yet, plenty of people do. Indeed, *BSBI News* itself uses them routinely. As do the aforementioned Wildflower Society, the magazine *British Wildlife* and Butterfly Conservation (for butterflies and for plants). The RHS and the RSPB, to their lasting credit, do not. The Bumblebee Conservation

Trust can't quite make up their mind. Is it Common Carder Bee or common carder bee? Neither, it's Common carder bee.

Here, for what it's worth, is the logic behind initial capitals, at least as reported by a correspondent in *BSBI News*: we need to remove the ambiguity between a small scabious (i.e. *any* vertically challenged scabious) and *the* Small Scabious (i.e. *Scabiosa columbaria*). Of course any competent writer will make sure their meaning is clear from the context, but if you really think the reader will be confused by a small scabious, what's wrong with a little scabious, or a short one? Or if it's really small, a tiny scabious, or a weak, starved, stunted or malnourished one?

So initial capitals are there to solve a problem that doesn't really exist. Instead they reveal a curious belief that the object of one's affections, whether a flower or a butterfly, is somehow special. In fact not just special, but Special. But at the same time a fear that this Specialness will be appreciated only if it is rammed home by capitalisation. But what if we all behaved like this? What if the Society of Greengrocers (which I just made up) started waxing lyrical about Leeks, Onions and Cauliflowers, and expected the rest of us to do the same?

Soon we either enter a Universe where every Noun and its Qualifier needs a Capital, just to be on the Safe Side (as distinct from a safe side), or we need such a complex set of rules to decide where capitals are needed and where they aren't that we need a Capitalisation Czar to keep us on the straight and narrow.

My advice? Stick to what they taught you in primary school: proper nouns start with capitals and everything else doesn't. Leave being Special to José Mourinho.

. . . . ✳ . . . .

Taxonomy of Meconopsis

It's not every day that a piece of information emerges from a research lab that makes you think 'Ha – so that's what's going on'. But I had such a eureka moment the other day when I came across some new work on the taxonomy of *Meconopsis*. I know we all have more important things to worry about, but surely I'm not the only gardener who has scratched his or her head over the strange behaviour of the different members of that genus. I hope we can all agree that the Himalayan blue poppies, beautiful as they are, are not the easiest plants to grow: downright picky, to be frank. In fact I've given up; my excuse, apart from sheer incompetence, is that my garden's just too dry. On the other hand, the one European member of the genus, Welsh poppy (*Meconopsis cambrica*) is simply a weed.

Interestingly, Linnaeus originally lumped Welsh poppy in with the other poppies in the genus *Papaver*. It was only later that someone decided it was different enough to have a genus to itself. Later still, when the Asiatic poppies were discovered, people thought they looked a lot like Welsh poppy (apart from being blue) and put them all in *Meconopsis*. But now a joint German–British–Spanish team, in research published in the *New Journal of Botany*, have looked at the DNA and got to the truth. Which is that Welsh poppy is indeed very closely related to poppies (i.e. *Papaver*) and not all closely related to the Asiatic *Meconopsis* species. In other words, Linnaeus was right all along (as he usually was), and the reason Welsh poppy and the blue poppies seem like chalk and cheese is because they are.

What does that do to the names of all these plants? Well, Welsh poppy is what is known in botanical jargon as the 'type' of *Meconopsis*, that is the plant on which the whole genus is founded, so technically it should stay put and all the blue poppies should become something else. But, recognising that this is a recipe for rioting in the streets, the researchers recommend that the Himalayan poppies stay where they are, and Welsh poppy finally goes where it started out, as *Papaver cambricum*.

True *Meconopsis* aficionados have always been deeply suspicious of Welsh poppy: 'This outlying species does not truly fit within the genus *Meconopsis*, and in time it is likely that this will be attended to by the botanists, with a name change' is the dismissive comment on www.meconopsis. org. They were right, and they were also right to be equally wary of a small group of Asiatic poppies with yellow flowers (*M. chelidonifolia*, *M. villosa* and *M. smithiana*), which turn out not to be closely related to the blue poppies, or to *Papaver*, or to anything else for that matter. The only solution for these plants is the genus *Cathcartia*: beautiful plants, but true to their *Meconopsis* heritage in being not all that easy to grow.

So the good news for any *Meconopsis* completists out there is that you can now eschew the undisciplined Welsh poppy with a clear conscience. The bad news, if like me you've always been baffled by the taxonomy within the Himalayan blue poppies, and never known which ones are perennial and which expire after flowering, is that the new research doesn't help. All it shows is that however many there may be (as few as 25, or maybe more than 50), all the blue poppies are indeed *very* closely related, so it's not surprising you can't tell them apart.

. . . . ❋ . . . .

Spelling mistakes

A few years ago I wrote a book about the science of gardening called *An Ear to the Ground*, in which I proposed *Ginkgo* as my candidate for the planet's most frequently misspelled plant name. As if to show just how easy this is, while checking the proofs of the paperback of *An Ear to the Ground* a few years later, I found that *I* had misspelled *Ginkgo* in the original hardback. Recently, *Ginkgo* was one of the stars of Richard Fortey's excellent BBC4 TV series *Survivors*, looking at various species that have managed to survive for unfeasibly long periods of time. And (I'm sure you can see where we're going here) when the name appeared on the screen, it was of course spelled wrongly.

All this prompted me to check up on how the world of *Ginkgo* misspelling had been getting on. Very well indeed, it turns out. When I first looked, nearly a decade ago, Google found millions of hits for *Ginkgo* and *Gingko*, but at least the correct spelling was in the majority. Today *Gingko* produces 24.6 million hits, while *Ginkgo* produces only 21 million. That's what I love about the internet – its ability to prove that all your worst fears were justified.

Ginkgo seems to be a very old name, originally from the Japanese *ginkyo*, but plant names based on names of people seem to be particularly prone to being spelled wrongly. The classic example, as every fule kno, is *Fuchsia*. Google finds

65.1 million hits for *Fuchsia*, but still a respectable 14.4 million hits for *Fuschia*. Admittedly, some of these do shake one's faith in the infallibility of Google itself. Top of the list is the website of the British Fuchsia Society, but try as I might, I can't find *Fuchsia* misspelled anywhere on their site. Maybe they've just cunningly arranged their website so that it can be found even by people who can't spell *Fuchsia*? Second up is Wikipedia, but only because it cautions that 'fuchsia is often misspelled as fuschia in English'. And I suspect, or at least I hope, that Fuschia Designs, Fuschia Events, Fuschia Beauty and Fuschia Dance are all just being deliberately ironic. Anyway, if spelling *Fuchsia* ever causes you problems, all you need to remember is that the genus is named after German botanist Leonhart Fuchs. Say 'fooksia' to yourself a few times and you'll never get it wrong.

How often *Aubrieta* is misspelled is impossible to tell, at least via Google. The problem here is that the genus is named after French flower-painter Claude Aubriet, but the correct generic name *Aubrieta* has never tripped off the tongue for English speakers. So the 'i' has tended to migrate, giving us the common English name of aubretia. Or sometimes an extra 'i' has appeared, giving us aubrietia. Google finds 900,000 examples of *Aubrieta*, and 155,000 instances of aubretia, some of which are misspellings of the Latin name, but most are just the common English name. And surprisingly, since I always thought aubretia was the usual

English spelling, Google turns up 262,000 hits for aubrietia. Anyway, as usual the key to remembering the Latin is not to forget about old Claude, although how you spell the English name is apparently up to you. My Word spell-checker, I find while checking this, plumps for aubrietia.

Plenty of people have had plants named after them, but sometimes you probably wish they hadn't. For example, 19th-century German homeopathic doctor Clemens Maria Franz von Boenninghausen (*Boenninghausenia*), Czech physician Adam Zaluziansky von Zaluzian (*Zaluzianskya*), Danish botanist Morten Wormskjold (*Veronica wormskjoldii*) and Russian botanist Carl Maximowicz (*Weigela maximowiczii*). Finally, spare a thought for poor old *Paeonia mlokosewitschii*, which has the misfortune (for non-Polish speakers anyway) to be named after Polish botanist Ludwik Mlokosiewicz.

· · · · · · · ·✳· · · · · · · · ·

Artichokes or cardoons?

Confused by cardoons? Alarmed by artichokes? Don't worry, you're not alone. The RHS has awarded the statuesque cardoon (*Cynara cardunculus*) its Award of Garden Merit (AGM) as an ornamental plant, but its website also says 'other common names: globe artichoke'. On the other hand, if you actually search for 'globe artichoke' on the RHS website, you find *Cynara scolymus*, clearly a related but (apparently) different species. The *European Garden Flora*, which lists everything, also thinks that the cardoon and globe artichoke are different species. The *New Oxford Book of Food Plants* agrees. But Clive Stace's *New Flora of the British Isles* lists only *Cynara cardunculus*, with the following qualification: 'var. cardunculus (cardoon), spiny, young shoots blanched and eaten, and var. scolymus (globe artichoke), spineless, succulent receptacle and bases of flower bracts eaten.' By the way, although Stace is rarely wrong about anything, he is wrong about which bit of cardoons is (allegedly) edible – it's the leaf stalks, not the shoots.

My personal rule of thumb is if I see *Cynara* in a flower bed, it's a cardoon, if it's in a veg plot, it's a globe artichoke, but this is hardly a satisfactory state of affairs. Which is why I was pleased to see a paper in the journal *Annals of Botany*, from a team of Italian biologists, that aims to find out what is going on. For a start, they have no truck with the idea of two species; there's the cultivated cardoon and artichoke, and there's a wild cardoon, but they're all one species: *C. cardunculus*. In fact conventional wisdom says that there are *two* wild cardoons: the eastern variety, small and rather spiny, in Greece, Italy, France and North Africa, and the western variety, larger and less spiny, in Spain and Portugal.

The solution, as usual these days, is to look at the DNA of all these plants, so that's what they did. The results were complicated in detail, but simple enough in broad outline. The eastern wild cardoon is genetically distinct and is clearly the original wild plant, in fact the researchers conclude the whole complex probably originated in Sicily. The cultivated cardoon and artichoke were both derived from this plant long ago, indeed the domestication of the artichoke was well under way by Roman times. Artichokes are tradition-ally propagated vegetatively, with numerous varieties selected over the centuries, varying from small and early-flowering to larger and late-flowering. In Italy in particular there are many named varieties, often named after localities and some distinguishing feature, such as head colour (e.g. 'Bianco di Ostuni' and 'Nero di Castrignano'). The cardoon was domes-ticated later and is closer in appearance to the wild species; unlike the artichoke, it is traditionally raised from seed.

Cultivated cardoons and 'wild' western cardoons are genetically almost identical, and it seems very likely that the western cardoon is an escape from cultivation, and that the original wild cardoon was an exclusively eastern Mediterranean plant.

Now we know what all these plants are, we can continue to enjoy them in the garden. Cardoons are one of the most striking ornamental plants you can grow, and few plants are more attractive to bees. I've never met anyone who has tried eating them, and anyway it almost seems a waste of such an attractive plant. On the other hand, few vegetables are as delicious (in my opinion) as globe artichokes. Good for you, too – they're packed with antioxidant compounds such as polyphenols and flavonoids. If you fancy growing your own, it's probably worth growing a named, vegetatively propagated variety, which will almost certainly be better than a plant grown from seed.

Alternatively, you could get on a plane to Brindisi and try the real thing. Hard to imagine a better place to eat a 'Bianco di Ostuni' than Ostuni itself.

· · · · · · · ❋ · · · · · · · ·

Botany and Latin

Botany. The very word is enough to send most of us to sleep. Indeed so boring is the subject perceived to be that most universities no longer admit to having botany departments at all; the university here in Sheffield long ago decided it preferred the sexier *plant sciences*.

Part of the problem, surely, is the Latin. Before Carl Linnaeus tidied things up, every plant (and animal) had a long, descriptive Latin name, which was effectively a thumb-nail description. Thus the tomato was *Solanum caule inermi herbaceo, foliis pinnatis incisis*, meaning 'smooth-stemmed herbaceous solanum with incised pinnate leaves'. These long names weren't standardised and tended to change over time, so it was often hard to tell which plant was being referred to. Linnaeus didn't mind these long names, but he also pro-vided short versions, probably originally just to save paper; thus tomato became *Solanum lycopersicum*. Short, but still Latin, or at any rate modified to look like Latin; so-called Latin names can be in any language. *Petunia* is from a native Brazilian word for tobacco, and many names commemorate people: for example *Magnolia wilsonii* is named for French botanist Pierre Magnol and plant collector Ernest 'Chinese' Wilson.

Latin names will always be with us, but Latin also intrudes into plant naming in other ways. When a new species is first named and described, that description has traditionally had to be in Latin. The reason is simple – when Linnaeus wrote the rules, in the 18th century, Latin was the international language of science. These days, the rules are debated when the world's botanists gather every six years at the International Botanical Congress, and at the XVIII Congress in Melbourne, Australia in July 2011, delegates were in revolutionary mood. They decided that henceforth, instead of requiring a description in a language nobody speaks, they would allow a description in a language nearly everyone speaks. So from 1 January 2012, it's been permitted to describe a new species in Latin *or* in English.

Emboldened by this decision, the Congress pressed on with another reform, perhaps even more radical. Descriptions of new species have to be published where anyone, at least in principle, can read them – in practice, in a scientific journal. Until now, not only did that description have to be in Latin, it had to actually physically exist, at least on a library shelf somewhere. But increasingly, scientific journals exist only online. Certainly anyone starting a new journal today – and around two or three new journals are founded every *day* – wouldn't even consider the trouble and expense of publishing a print version. Even print versions of long-established journals increasingly exist only as a nod to tradition, and the day isn't far off when print copies of journals will be as rare as vinyl records. Thus the Congress found itself facing a time, not far in the future, when it would be difficult to validly publish a description of a new species, because the required hard copy would no longer exist. To allow new names to be published electronically had already been proposed and rejected at previous meetings, but this time Congress bowed to the inevitable.

It seems that even for botany, the times are a-changing. With one mighty lurch, botanical nomenclature has dragged itself from the 18th into the 21st century. That still doesn't exactly make botany cool, of course, but at least quill pen and parchment are no longer required. So although finding the estimated 20 per cent of plant species that haven't been discovered yet hasn't got any easier, telling everyone about it when we do has.

Not surprisingly, taxonomists were queuing up to take advantage of the new rules, and the first new plant to be described online, in English, was a new species of *Solanum* from South Africa. It's related to the aubergine, but the description doesn't tell us what it tastes like. And just to bring us right up to date, three new species of Brazilian *Solanum* were described (online, in English) only two weeks ago. Good job the botanists from the Universidade Federal de Minas Gerais in Belo Horizonte got that out of the way – I'm sure they've other things on their minds for the next few weeks.*

. . . .✳. . . . .

---

* This was published during the 2014 football World Cup in Brazil. Some of the games were played in Belo Horizonte.

The European Garden Flora

If you see a plant you don't recognise, what are your options? If you're out in the countryside, where your plant has a good chance of being a native, or at least a well-naturalised alien, there's a cornucopia of wildflower books to help you. Most have photographs or coloured illustrations, and since the UK flora is pretty small, you're quite likely to find your plant by just working your way through the pictures. If you want to be a bit more scientific about it, you can use a book with an *identification key* – a sequence of questions that will lead you (if you're careful) to the right answer. The best book on the UK flora for the keen amateur – by a wide margin – is *The Wild Flower Key* (Revised Edition) by Francis Rose and Clare O'Reilly, published by Warne in 2006. This splendid book, which I cannot recommend too highly, has a friendly key *and* super illustrations. Serious botanical geeks, on the other hand, will use Clive Stace's *New Flora of the British Isles*, which is comprehensive and big, but hard work. If you can't find a plant in 'Stace', as it is universally known, you're just not trying, because – trust me – it's in there somewhere.

But suppose you see a *garden* plant you don't recognise? Now what do you do? Sit down to look at the thousands of pictures in the *RHS Book of Perennials* (or whatever) until you see one that looks similar? Phone a friend? Serious plant people can get quite a long way with Stace, since he includes not only the native flora but also almost every introduction, however uncommon, that has ever escaped into the wild. Since most of these plants started out in gardens, you might find what you're looking for. But chances are you won't, because most garden plants are not found in the wild at all.

Once upon a time, that was the end of the road, because there just wasn't a book that allowed the serious plantaholic to identify any garden plant. Then along came *The European Garden Flora*, published by Cambridge University Press. It took sixteen years to complete, in six volumes published at various times between 1984 and 2000. Its subtitle is *A manual for the identification of plants cultivated in Europe, both out-of-doors and under glass*, and it does what it says on the tin. I've no idea how many plants are in there, and I'm not sure anyone else has either. The authors began with everything in every European nursery catalogue, i.e. everything you could actually *buy* (well over 12,000 species), and then added everything else they could find. The only plants they left out were real curiosities that you could expect to find only in one or two botanical gardens, so if you're stumped by one of them, let's hope it has a label.

Why am I telling you this? Because there's now a lovely new, fully revised second edition, and by leaving out the conifers and ferns this time, they've managed to get the whole thing down to a mere five volumes, 3,472 pages, 9.7 kg and – apart from a few line drawings – no pictures. Your next birthday may be a little way off, but if you ask nicely now, that gives your nearest and dearest plenty of time to save up the £699 needed to buy it. And it gives *you* plenty of time to put up the new shelves needed for when it arrives.

. . . . ❋ . . . .

Herbaceous borders

We spend a lot of time admiring them, talking about them, plotting their construction, even reading books about them. Herbaceous borders, that is. But what is a herbaceous border? Or, to boil that question down to its essentials, since we're unlikely to disagree about 'border', what do we mean by 'herbaceous'?

I confess that's a question to which the answer has always seemed so obvious it had never occurred to me to be worth asking until the other day. But reading an article in *The Garden*, extolling the virtues of plants that hold on to their leaves in winter, I came across this statement: 'herbaceous perennials are deciduous, dying to the ground in winter'.

Is that right? Here's my *Shorter Oxford Dictionary* on the subject: 'herbaceous: not forming a woody stem but dying down to the root each year'. The *RHS Dictionary of Gardening* says something very similar. Trouble is, there are two ideas there, and they're not only quite separate but more or less unrelated: 'not woody' and 'dying down to the root each year'. If we keep 'herbaceous' to mean both of them, then I think that leaves us without a word for all those plants that are non-woody but do *not* die down to the root each year. There is no shortage of such plants; almost all our common native grasses for a start. Which is just as well, for were it not so, the lawn in winter really would be a sorry sight. In fact, in a world in which grasses were generally deciduous, it's hard to believe that the lawn would ever have been invented.

If I understand correctly, *The Garden*'s suggested name for all those non-woody plants that keep their leaves in winter is 'wintergreen perennials'. But 'wintergreen' comes with too much baggage for my liking. It's already (a) several rare but beautiful native woodland wildflowers in the genera *Pyrola* and *Orthilia*, and (b) North American shrub *Gaultheria procumbens* and the aromatic oil extracted from its leaves. I don't think wintergreen will catch on, and the world might be a simpler place if it doesn't. If we do have to keep 'wintergreen', maybe it would be a useful word for those plants, like *Cyclamen hederifolium*, that have leaves *only* in the winter.

Instead, I'm inclined to go with *The European Garden*

Flora, for whom a herbaceous plant is just one 'in which the stems do not become woody'. Thus 'herbaceous' is simply defined as the opposite of woody, and the two ideas that the *Garden* definition needlessly conflates are usefully kept apart: plants can be woody or herbaceous, and both can be either deciduous or evergreen. The argument about whether palms or bamboos are truly woody can be left for another day.

So bergenias, hellebores, sedges, pulmonarias, saxifrages, most heucheras, many euphorbias and epimediums, several ferns and geraniums, *Ophiopogon*, *Libertia peregrinans*, *Stachys byzantina* and many more can all be readmitted as *bona fide* members of the herbaceous border. In these modern, enlightened times, probably a few shrubs too, but that's another argument we don't need to have right now.

By the way, the noun that goes with herbaceous is herb, and to a botanist a herb is just any non-woody plant. Confusingly, herbs in the culinary or medicinal sense can be either herbaceous or woody.

GROWING
FOOD

Allotment soil

Soil is one of the great failures of modern intensive agriculture. Healthy soils, beneath natural grasslands and – especially – woodlands, contain lots of organic matter. That organic matter holds on to nutrients and gives the soil structural stability, allowing it to resist damage by, for example, heavy rain, thus preventing soil erosion. There's also plenty of life in a healthy soil, lots of burrowing earthworms, and so lots of pore space too. A healthy soil is basically a giant sponge, which fills up with water after rain, gradually releasing that water to plants in dry weather.

When land is cleared for agriculture, and especially for arable crops, all that goes out of the window. The organic matter in arable soils is lost to the atmosphere as CO_2, and the soil loses its structure and strength, leading to compaction and erosion. Arable soils also lose their ability to hold on to water, nutrients and pollutants, leaking nutrients into groundwater and lakes and rivers, causing eutrophication and, if the water is for human use, the need for expensive water treatment.

Although this is all depressingly well-known, the conventional view is that all this soil degradation is the price we have to pay for the high yields of arable crops on which we all depend. But, says new research just published in the *Journal of Applied Ecology*, gardening proves the conventional view to be completely wrong. The researchers looked at the properties of soils on allotments in Leicester, along with those from other urban sites, and compared them with soils beneath arable fields and pasture in the countryside around Leicester.

The arable soils showed all the usual symptoms: compacted, lifeless and low in organic matter. Allotment soils, by contrast, were more open, more fertile, and higher in organic matter, in fact they weren't all that different from soils beneath woodland. The reason isn't hard to find: composting of allotment waste is virtually universal among allotment holders, most also import household green waste as well, and use of manure and other kinds of commercial compost is widespread. In short, soils on allotments are healthy because allotment holders go to a lot of trouble to keep them that way.

Nor are these healthy soils any barrier to high yields. During the Second World War 'Dig for Victory' campaign, allotments and gardens provided around 10 per cent of food consumed in the UK, despite covering less than 1 per cent of the area of arable cultivation. Recent research also shows that gardens and allotments produce yields of fruit and vegetables four to eleven times greater than conventional agricultural crops. In fact, soil organic matter is now so low beneath many agricultural soils that it makes it increasingly hard to maintain high crop yields.

These results are not unique to allotments; soils in private gardens were pretty good too. In fact garden soils beneath trees and shrubs were the best of all, presumably because they are undisturbed and also benefit from the organic matter added by fallen leaves. Nevertheless, allotments are unique in the way they manage to combine a productive 'agricultural' function (i.e. growing food) with healthy soils.

The policy lessons are clear, but I'll spell them out anyway. Encouraging people to grow their own food simultaneously targets food security, improves the well-known (physical and psychological) health benefits of gardening, and helps to reduce climate change, flooding, pollution and erosion. You seriously want to save the planet? Give us the tools, and the land, and we – gardeners – will do it for you.

. . . .❋. . . . .

Cabbage patch, part I

Growing scattered along the sea cliffs of southern England, and in similar habitats throughout South-West Europe and the Mediterranean, is a rather nondescript yellow-flowered member of the cabbage family – the crucifers or Brassicaceae. It is none other than wild cabbage, *Brassica oleracea.* The green-fingered genius who saw in this unattractive weed the potential to give rise to a whole greengrocer's full of vegetables is unknown, but there ought to be a monument to him (or more likely her) somewhere. Like many vegetables, cabbage is a biennial, albeit not a very strict one that often lingers on into perenniality. The variety that remains closest to the ancestral wild cabbage, and also tastes the worst in the opinion of many, is kale or collards. Kale doesn't do much except grow lots of leaves, which are eaten in the spring. Its main virtue is that it's very hardy and can produce a crop at a time when the vegetable garden has very little else to offer. 'Cabbage', in all its various Savoy, spring and red forms, was developed in Germany between the 12th and 16th centuries. Brussels sprouts are also not too far from the original species, differing only in the production of enlarged, axillary winter buds, each like a tiny cabbage. Surprisingly, sprouts were the last variety of cabbage to be developed, first appearing near Brussels in the middle of the 18th century.

While gardeners in Germany were pushing the boundaries of cabbage leaves, Italian gardeners were having a go at the flowers. Sprouting broccoli is closest to the ancestral form, and produces loose clusters of white or purple flower heads in spring. You get something very similar (except green) if you just let old Brussels sprout plants flower in the spring. At the opposite extreme, cauliflower produces a single, swollen head of undeveloped flowers (yes, as Mark Twain observed, cauliflower really is nothing but cabbage with a college education), while calabrese is intermediate, with a large green terminal head, but also a few extra side shoots. Compared to sprouting broccoli, the attraction of calabrese from a commercial perspective is that it doesn't need to overwinter but matures in the summer and autumn.

So much for leaves and flowers, but not to be outdone, the possibilities of the cabbage stem are realised in the shape of kohl rabi, in which the lower part of the stem is swollen into a turnip-like globe. Of all cabbage's manifestations, kohl rabi is arguably the most underrated, and also probably both the easiest to grow and the fastest to produce a usable crop from sowing.

It's probably fair to say that although the great age of vegetable invention is over, adventurous seed companies haven't given up tinkering with cabbage. British company Tozer has developed what is claimed to be the first really new vegetable for a decade. This hybrid of kale and Brussels sprouts produces little frilly leaf rosettes all the way up the stem, and is supposed to be as hardy as kale, while milder and sweeter than sprouts. After much thought, they've called it a flower sprout, and the first variety 'petit posy'. It could have been much worse – krouts, anyone? Meanwhile, plant and seed merchants Thompson & Morgan have been crossing calabrese with kai-lan or Chinese kale to produce a plant that they've almost inevitably decided to call 'brokali'. Clearly there's life in the old cabbage yet.

Given the enormous potential of cabbage stems, leaves and flowers to give rise to almost every imaginable form of vegetable, you might wonder why cabbage seeds and roots have been ignored as potential crops. The reason is simple – cabbage has close relatives where these possibilities have been exploited to their full (and confusing) potential. But that's another story.

. . . .❋. . . . .

Cabbage patch, part II

If I told you there are two very similar large, yellow-flowered brassicas, *Brassica napus* and *B. rapa*, and that only one of them is rape (canola in North America), I guess you would be disappointed to hear that it's *B. napus*, and not *B. rapa*. As the official crucifer book says drily of *B. napus*: 'much confused with *B. rapa*, not least due to confusion between the English and Latin names'. In fact, if I'm not mistaken, you're feeling confused about them already, aren't you? To add to the confusion, rape isn't even a proper species – it's almost certainly originally a hybrid between *B. oleracea* (cabbage) and *B. rapa*, and exists only in cultivation. Despite being unknown as a genuine wild plant, rape is now very common in the wild as an escape from cultivation, not least because no other plant is quite so likely to have fallen (literally) off the back of a lorry.

How do we know this? Well, Professor Mick Crawley from Imperial College London noticed that there seemed to be an awful lot of rape growing on the verges of the M25 motorway, but that individual patches of rape are short-lived, disappearing almost as quickly as they appear. This is hardly surprising, since rape is an annual and cannot easily establish from seed in competition with the rank perennial vegetation that normally grows on motorway verges. It's clear that rape establishes after soil disturbance, especially after roadworks, but then dies out over the next year or two.

But where does it come from? Two possibilities seemed likely: either the soil seed bank, or invasion from crops growing near the motorway. But investigation quickly revealed that rape does not have a soil seed bank, and that its distribution on the M25 verge is unrelated to rape growing in nearby fields. So, there was no evidence that the rape was surviving in the soil or invading from adjacent agricultural land.

Crawley then had a brainwave – there was something very odd about the distribution of rape patches (at this point, it might be helpful to go and get a road atlas before reading on). North of the junction for Erith, just south of the Dartford tunnel, almost all rape grew on the clockwise (outer) verge. South of the Erith junction, almost all rape grew on the anti-clockwise verge. The significance of this finding is that the largest oilseed rape crushing plant in Britain, consuming around half the rape grown here, is at Erith. The clear implication is that rape seed is spilling from laden lorries travelling to Erith. North of the river, such lorries will be travelling clockwise, while south of the river they will be travelling in the opposite direction.

The late, great Linda Smith came from Erith and used to joke that it wasn't twinned with anywhere, but did have a suicide pact with Dagenham. She also claimed that her home town was the most boring place in Britain. But clearly for *Brassica* fanciers it isn't, and I just thought it was time to set the record straight.

Anyway, not content with mixing up their Latin and English names so that no one can remember which is which, *B. rapa* and *B. napus* have another trick up their sleeves. The familiar *B. napus* cultivar, bred for its oil-rich seeds, and which now turns so much of Britain yellow in early summer, is rape. But there is another *B. napus* cultivar bred for its swollen root. The origins of this form are a mystery, but it was originally popular in Scandinavia and spread from there to the rest of Europe, hence the name Swedish turnip, or swede for short. If you're confused by swedes and turnips, that's hardly surprising, since *B. rapa* is the familiar turnip. Neither swede nor turnip escapes from cultivation much, unlike rape, although the *wild* turnip (lacking the swollen root) is a common wild plant.

And now a question for connoisseurs of trivia: if presented with a turnip and a swede, how could you be sure of telling them apart? The key is that although both are swollen roots, the turnip is *only* root, while the swede also incorporates the lower part of the stem, and since the diagnostic feature of stems is the possession of leaves, a swede always has several concentric ridges near the top, which are the attachment scars of leaves. Turnips, on the other hand, are quite smooth. Simples, eh?

· · · · · · ·�֍· · · · · · · ·

Growing food to reduce your carbon footprint

I hope we agree that gardening is good for you, whatever you decide to grow. Indeed, a fair case can be made for the value of just sipping a gin and tonic while watching the weeds grow. But, I would also submit, the very highest level of satisfaction comes from growing at least some of your own food. Quite apart from the fresh air and exercise involved in the actual cultivation, and the health benefits of eating your own fresh produce, the environmentally aware gardener will be chuffed by reducing a few food miles, and thus doing her bit to save the planet.

But, if the latter consideration is important to you, what should you grow? Specifically, what will lower your food-related carbon footprint the most? This is no joke: the growing, transportation, packaging, retailing and cooking of food, together with the clearing of land to grow food in the first place, accounts for as much as 30 per cent of the UK's carbon footprint. A recent paper in the journal *Landscape and Urban Planning* considered this question, specifically in the context of urban community farms, but the principles apply equally to the private gardener.

A key consideration, not surprisingly, is yield – all things being equal, you're better off growing high-yielding crops than low-yielding ones. So courgettes, for example, which are both high-yielding and almost entirely imported, are a good choice. But yield isn't everything: potatoes are almost all grown in the UK and their carbon footprint is small, so little is gained (in CO_2 terms) by growing your own. Sometimes yield outweighs other concerns. So although it takes a lot of energy (and therefore CO_2 emissions) to manufacture a greenhouse or polytunnel, the much higher yield of greenhouse-grown tomatoes more than compensates for that. Tomatoes are also mostly imported, and even those grown in the UK mostly come from heated green-houses that use a lot of energy. Strawberries, on the other hand, are not worth growing in a polytunnel – at least not to save CO_2 emissions – because yields are much lower than tomatoes.

Sometimes the CO_2 emissions from transport are of primary importance. Exhibit A here is green beans, which are imported year-round in large quantities by the UK from outside Europe, mostly from Kenya. Only in mid- to late summer do UK-grown beans make a dent in our imports. Because the beans are imported by air, their carbon footprint is huge, making it very worthwhile to grow your own. Here, however, the arguments start to get more complicated. First, 'CO_2-saving' depends on the assumption that your own produce directly substitutes for (imported) produce from the supermarket. But if you care about your carbon footprint, maybe you wouldn't consider buying beans air-freighted from Africa in the first place? In which case, your CO_2 saving is more notional, and depends on the carbon footprint of what you *would* eat (if you weren't growing your own). Plus, there's always the difficulty of the welfare of the 2 million Kenyans who depend on us to buy their fruit, flowers and vegetables.

But if we grow all the right things, how well are we doing, relatively speaking? That all depends on what you choose to compare it with. Planting trees soaks up CO_2, but growing your own fruit and veg does much better, in fact about ten times better, than planting trees on the same land. On the other hand, most of the emissions of CO_2 (and other greenhouse gases) from food come from the production and consumption of meat and dairy products. If you gave up eating meat, or significantly reduced your consumption, your carbon footprint would be greatly improved, almost irrespective of where your fruit and veg came from.

· · · · · · ·❋· · · · · · · ·

The raspberry manifesto

I can see why some people aren't attracted by growing veg; after all, you do need a few proper tools, various parts of the process can be cold/wet/muddy, a lot can go wrong, and there is always the possibility of everything being eaten by slugs. But growing your own fruit? Nothing, I submit, could be simpler. For maximum versatility and ease, I could make a case for gooseberries, but in fact I'm going to try to convince you – if you don't already – to grow raspberries. To make my point, my 'raspberry manifesto' compares them with their chief rival for the affections of the would-be soft fruit grower, the strawberry.

- Strawberries are back-breaking to pick. Raspberries grow at a convenient chest height.

- If your garden is at all prone to slugs, you will soon discover that strawberries are near the top of their list of tasty treats. The dedicated strawberry grower spends a lot of time propping up the fruit on dry straw in an attempt to keep them out of the way of mud and slugs. Raspberries are above all that.

- Yields from strawberry plants decline rapidly as the plants age. The great Hessayon says strawberries have a useful life of three to five years, while the RHS recommends replacing plants after three years. Commercial growers, for whom high yields are crucial, often replace their plants every year. Raspberries, on the other hand, are immortal. Various sources say plants begin to go downhill after eight to twelve years, but this is eyewash – my patch, planted twenty years ago, produced as good a crop as ever last year, and shows every sign of carrying on for ever.

- If you don't net strawberries, they really are just an elaborate way of feeding the birds. Summer-fruiting raspberries may also suffer badly from predation by birds, but they may not, and in any case there is a way round the problem.

⟠ If you think there is a finer summery pud than raspberry pavlova, then I'm afraid I shall have to ask you to step outside. Also, if you haven't tried Scottish delicacy cranachan, then believe me it's time you did. There are many variations on the recipe, but essentially it's just all your favourite Scottish ingredients – toasted oatmeal, whisky, raspberries, heather honey and cream – mixed or layered together. Yum. The only thing missing is haggis, but I'm sure Heston Blumenthal could fix that.

⟠ 'Framboise', performed by Boby Lapointe in Truffaut's *Shoot the Piano Player* (*Tirez sur le pianiste*) is easily the best song in French New Wave cinema. Not exactly a crowded field, you may argue, and I would have to agree, but no one ever wrote a song half as good about strawberries. You can find it on YouTube, but the whole film is worth watching.

The most popular raspberry varieties are summer-fruiting. Like their close relative the blackberry, the canes are essentially biennial, growing one year and fruiting the next. Thus fruit are produced in summer, following on directly from (or somewhat overlapping with) the strawberry season. But there is another type of raspberry that fruits in autumn, and this is the one I'm going to try to persuade you to grow, for several reasons:

⁊ Summer raspberries are simple enough to grow, but there's always that slightly awkward moment when you have to cut down the fruited canes, while leaving the new canes to fruit next year. Hard to get this wrong, but at the same time surprisingly easy, crawling around with secateurs in hand, to accidentally snip through a new cane. But autumn raspberries grow and fruit in a single season, then you cut the whole lot down, and new ones grow. What could be simpler? Nothing, that's what. Gardening books generally recommend that the old canes are cut down in late winter, but why, for heaven's sake? The tradition in the Thompson garden is to pick the last raspberries on 5 November, cut down the canes and throw them straight on the annual bonfire. Job done, and now nothing to do until you start picking again in the following August.

⁊ The RHS recommends tying in canes individually to a wire support, and summer-fruiting varieties certainly need this, because the canes have to survive winter gales. Here again, however, autumn varieties are easier – I just have a length of old washing line tied round posts at the four corners of my row, and that's all the support they need. But grow short, sturdy 'Autumn Bliss' in a sheltered spot, and you may well manage without any support at all. One thing's for sure – the elaborate structure you may have seen Monty Don using for his raspberries on *Gardeners' World* is quite unnecessary for the autumn variety.

- The main reason you're advised to replace raspberry canes every ten years or so is a build-up of viruses and other diseases. But autumn varieties tend to be disease-free, since the long period with no canes helps to reduce the 'bridge' between seasons that keeps diseases going from one year to the next.

- Autumn raspberries are out of sync with the dreaded raspberry beetle, so it's rare to find maggots in your fruit.

- Raspberries tend to be less damaged by birds than strawberries anyway, and autumn varieties are particularly trouble-free; bird damage to my raspberries is negligible.

There is, of course, nothing to stop you growing summer *and* autumn raspberries, guaranteeing an almost continuous supply from July to October. But a word of caution: take care where you plant them. Both types have remarkable powers of spread via underground runners, so unless you plant the different varieties a long way apart, they have an alarming tendency to get mixed up. Once this happens, all is lost, because it's no longer possible to know what (or when) to prune. On the other hand, this very free production of runners makes them very easy to propagate, so as long as you have a friend or relative who grows raspberries, you shouldn't need to buy any. Who said there was no such thing as a free lunch?

. . . . ✳ . . . .

Students growing
their own

Gardening is one of those things that we tend to take more seriously in later life, perhaps because that's when many of us own our own homes and have a bit more spare time. At the opposite end of the age spectrum, strenuous efforts are being made to interest children in gardening, not least by the Royal Horticultural Society.

Between those two ends of the age range, it's sometimes assumed that there is less interest in gardening. And yet university students ought to be receptive to the idea of gardening, or at least of growing your own food. They are (relatively) poor, not short of spare time, and are yet to have their idealism crushed by banks, politicians and the Inland Revenue. In other words, they may be slightly more likely than the rest of us to care about organic food, sustainability and food miles.

So full marks to the National Union of Students for supporting the Student Eats project. And congratulations to the students from Walsall College and Staffordshire, Reading and Roehampton Universities who are taking the project to the new Discovery Zone at RHS Chelsea Flower Show.

The idea originated at the University of Exeter in 2012, when a team of students turned a patch of land on the edge of the campus into a community garden to produce low-carbon, organic food. With funding from the Big Lottery's Local Food Fund, Student Eats spread to seventeen other institutions in 2013, with a further five joining this year. I checked if my university – Sheffield – is involved, and they are. Not only that, I also found they were just about (next day in fact) to have an open day to promote the project, so I pottered over there to see what they were up to.

I found the Lottery money had been invested in some splendid timber raised beds, three enormous concrete compost bins, a tool shed and a greenhouse, the guttering of which feeds two water butts. The beds are full of peas, broad beans, spring onions, fennel, herbs, chard, carrots and lettuce – lots and lots of lettuce in fact. In the greenhouse, trays of basil and leeks are waiting to be planted. The students who look after the plots are beginners, more or less by definition, but they're learning fast. Last year (their first) they grew courgettes, but this veg-plot staple doesn't really fit with the student year: so this year, no courgettes. They also found that nothing beats kohl rabi – a much under-rated crop in my opinion – for a huge crop in a short space of time. But they also found that no one actually wanted to eat most of it: so this year, no kohl rabi. Hence this year's mammoth lettuce crop – it grows fast, and everybody likes lettuce. There's also, as in any organisation basically run by committee, the occasional failure of communication. A row of parsnips were about three feet tall, and just about to flower; someone had remembered to sow them last year, but no one had remembered to harvest and eat them.

There's fruit too; nearby plots had rhubarb, blackcur-rants, redcurrants, gooseberries and blueberries. To help pollination, local beekeepers will install a hive later this year. No apples, but a helpful local apple expert alerted them to the apple trees growing around the nearby student accom-modation, so they helped themselves and turned the apples into chutney, apple butter and other yummy stuff (which they promptly ate).

I also have to report that at the open day, a quid bought me a large cup of Fairtrade tea and a super slice of beetroot and chocolate cake (and that the paper cup, napkin and teabag were promptly recycled, as they should be, via the compost heap).

In the end I had to conclude that if this is how even a few of the next generation are choosing to spend their time, the future is in safer hands than I thought.

········ ✳ ········

Bees and strawberries

More than three-quarters of the world's crop species are dependent to some extent on pollination by animals, over-whelmingly bees. If there were no bees, you wouldn't starve, because the crops that provide most of our calories don't depend on bees. But life without bees would be awfully dull; you would basically be left with bread, potatoes, rice and pasta. It would also be very unhealthy; nearly all our vitamins and other essential nutrients come from bee-pollinated plants.

So without bees about one-third of global crop production – and by far the most interesting and tasty third – just wouldn't be there. Which is bad enough, but new research shows that we owe bees even more than that: many crops don't just depend on bees for sheer tonnage, they're also *better* with bees around.

In research reported in the *Proceedings of the Royal Society*, researchers in Germany grew nine strawberry cultivars, including all the usual favourites like Elsanta and Honeoye. Nearby beehives and artificial nests for solitary bees made sure there were plenty of bees about. Some of the strawberries were covered with a very fine mesh, fine enough to exclude even pollen, so these strawberries could only be self-pollinated. Others were covered with a mesh that excluded insects, allowing the possibility of wind pollination, while others were uncovered. Fruits were harvested and sorted into commercial grades following the official trade guidelines; strawberry value depends a lot on appearance, and fruits that are small or have aberrations in shape or colour are worth much less. They also measured fruit firmness; firmer strawberries keep better, so they're worth more. Finally, they also measured sugar and acid content.

You will not be surprised to hear that on the basis of anything and everything that can be measured, bee-pollinated strawberries were better. They were bigger, brighter red, had fewer misshapen fruits, were firmer and kept better, and had the best sugar:acid ratio. Self-pollinated strawberries were worst of all, in other words wind pollination helped a bit, but not a lot. The researchers estimate that bees contribute around half of the value of the European strawberry crop on *quality* grounds alone, quite apart from any effect on yield.

The reasons for the differences in fruit quality became obvious when the researchers counted the number of fertilised seeds per strawberry (the seeds are the small pips on the surface of the fruit). Fertilised seeds produce hormones that help the fruit to grow and improve its quality, and bee-pollinated plants had far more fertilised seeds. Seeds that don't get fertilised don't make these hormones, resulting in poor-quality, malformed fruit.

Given that commercial beehives were kept near the field where the strawberries were grown, the researchers were surprised to discover that two-thirds of visits to strawberry flowers were made by wild bees, especially solitary *Osmia bicornis*, the red mason bee. As many other researchers have discovered, there is a limit to what can be achieved with honey bees alone – if you want pollination done properly, there's really no substitute for a healthy population of wild bees.

Home gardeners often pay rather little attention to the keeping qualities of the fruit and vegetables they grow; fruit in particular sometimes doesn't even make it back to the kitchen, so how long it keeps isn't really important. But this new research adds to a growing body of work showing that effective pollination improves the quality of everything from blueberries to cucumbers and tomatoes. Given that in the so-called 'developed' world, up to a half of fruit and vegetables are lost soon after harvest owing to damage and deterioration during handling, transport and storage, or wasted later on by retailers and consumers, anything that improves keeping quality has got to be a good thing. One more reason – as if one were needed – to look after our wild bees.

. . . . ❋ . . . .

Nutritious vegetables

What decides what you grow to eat in your garden? It may be what tastes best, or it may just be just what grows with the least effort; it's certainly hard to resist the sheer bounteousness of courgettes, even if they're not your favourite vegetable.

Another consideration, although perhaps one that won't have occurred to most of us, is the ability of different plants to deliver the essential nutrients you need for a healthy diet. A recent paper in the *Journal of the Academy of Nutrition and Dietetics* looked at this question, using the Nutrient Rich Foods (NRF) index. For each food, the NRF index simply adds up all the per cent daily values (per serving) for nine 'good' nutrients you want to eat more of, then subtracts the sum of per cent daily values for three 'bad' nutrients most of us eat too much of.

'Daily values' are worked out by the US Food and Drug Administration, but are similar to the UK's 'Guideline Daily

Amounts'. The nine 'good' nutrients are protein, fibre, vitamins A, C and E, calcium, magnesium, potassium and iron, while the three bad guys are the usual suspects: saturated fat, sugar and salt. The more of the former and the less of the latter, the higher a food scores.

If we look just at vegetables, very near the top are 'dark green' vegetables of all kinds, including leafy salads, chard, cabbage and broccoli. The king of healthy veg, an excellent source of nearly everything, is spinach. If maximising healthy nutrients per square yard is your aim, these are the things your veg plot should be full of.

Next come squashes, pumpkins and carrots, closely followed by a large group of 'other vegetables' (including asparagus, beetroot, cauliflower, green beans, iceberg lettuce, courgettes, onions and turnips); all still good for you, but not quite up there with cabbage. All these vegetables are slightly better for you raw than cooked, largely owing to the loss of vitamins and minerals on cooking.

Next come potatoes, although here there's a lot of variation in how you choose to eat them; baked or boiled, sadly, is much better for you than chips. Interestingly, sweet potatoes have the highest NRF index of all, above even leafy vegetables; sweet potatoes are a particularly good source of vitamins and also of potassium, which is good for your blood pressure. So the definitive answer to whether potatoes count as one of your five a day is no, but sweet potatoes do.

It's just a pity that, despite new hardier cultivars becoming available, sweet potatoes are still not all that easy to grow in the UK.

But don't get too carried away by differences between individual vegetables. If we take a step back and look at the bigger picture, all fruit and veg have high NRF scores. Dry beans, pulses, nuts and seeds have similarly high scores. Both outscore meat because although it has plenty of useful nutrients, meat is let down by lack of fibre and high levels of saturated fat. A bit below meat comes eggs, then dairy products and grains, and finally (with *negative* nutrient scores) pure processed things like sugar and fats. In short, compared to all the other things you could be eating, any fruit and veg is a healthy option, and of course growing them is itself good for you.

Finally, I forgot to mention tomatoes, which better than anything illustrate that exactly how you consume some foods makes all the difference. Tomatoes have a moderately high NRF score and are definitely one of your five a day, but cooked tomatoes aren't as good as raw or juice, and most shop-bought pasta sauces are no better for you than a bacon sandwich.

· · · · · · ·✳· · · · · · · ·

Breeding for flavour

Breeding – of both fruit and vegetables – concentrates primarily on yield, closely followed by good resistance to damage during harvest, shipping and storage. Not surprisingly, everything else, including nutrient content and flavour, has tended to go by the board, particularly since the Second World War. In fact flavour is the real Cinderella here, since not only is it hard to measure objectively, there is no agreement on the 'ideal' taste.

Happily, things may just be starting to change. Increasingly unimpressed by dull, bland fruit and vegetables, a growing number of consumers are willing to pay a premium for better flavour. At the same time, improving technology is beginning to allow plant breeders to measure and manipulate flavour, although there's still a long way to go; most of the thousands of chemicals found in a mature tomato, for example, are still unidentified. A lot of recent research has focused on tomatoes, where the foundation of good flavour is plenty of sugars and acids, present in the right proportions to give a good balance between sweet and sour. The same applies to many other fruits, for example strawberries, but not all; muskmelons are basically just sweet with very little acid, and a major aim of melon breeding is simply more sugar. Even this simple objective, however, has proved elusive, since it turns out to be difficult to break the link between sugar content and size: sweeter melons are smaller.

Much effort has been devoted to increasing sugar and acid content in tomatoes, but flavour consists of far more than that. The human mouth can detect only five basic flavours, and most of the sensation of flavour comes from smell, which is why food tastes of nothing when you have a cold. In tomatoes the key to flavour is around 400 aromatic, volatile chemicals, although only about twenty have a big impact on flavour. Broadly, these important flavour chemicals fall into three groups. The so-called C6 (six carbon atoms) volatiles are among the most abundant, and provide the green, grassy notes that also make tomato leaves smell the way they do. Interestingly, these chemicals decline in ripe fruits and some are lost if tomatoes are skinned. To put them back, and give your tomato sauce that straight-off-the-vine flavour, add a couple of tomato leaves near the end of cooking, but remove before eating (think bay leaves). Clever Italian chefs have been doing this for years without telling the rest of us.

A second set of tomato flavour chemicals are made from carotenoids (antioxidants like vitamin A) and are important in the flavour of many foods, from citrus to saffron. Humans can detect these floral/fruity scents at very low concentrations, and they are only synthesised at the very last stage of ripening, so they provide a good guide to full ripeness. The third group are made from amino acids and confer pleasant floral aromas; one of the main tomato chemicals is also the major constituent of rose scent.

These three groups don't come close to exhausting the possibilities of fruit flavours. In strawberries the main flavour chemicals are esters and furanones. Esters are very widespread and account for lots of common fruity aromas. They're important in pear, banana and pineapple and one – isoamyl acetate – is used to make pear drops taste (a bit) like pears. Another – ethyl acetate – is commonly used as nail varnish remover. Furanones contribute to the flavour of raspberry and pineapple, but many furanones are not fruity at all. Some are produced during cooking or fermentation and add meaty or nutty/spicy flavours; the taste of beer and soy sauce owe a lot to furanones.

We know much more than we did ten years ago about flavour, but is this helping to make better-tasting fruit? Well, sometimes, although much of the effort to engineer flavour is still little more than trial and error. You can't just assume that more flavour must be better. For example, tomatoes contain small amounts of methylsalicylate, aka oil of wintergreen, but too much of that makes tomatoes taste like Germolene. Even increasing chemicals that everyone agrees smell nice doesn't necessarily work. American researchers engineered tomatoes to make more of a group of volatiles that all come from the amino acid phenylalanine.

Consumers had no trouble distinguishing them from 'normal' tomatoes, but weren't sure they actually liked them any better. Genetic engineering also makes it possible to introduce completely new flavours, although whether this is always a good idea is debatable. Maybe with one eye on the pesto market, another group of researchers engineered tomatoes to make the terpenoids that give basil its characteristic flavour. Again, consumers had no trouble detecting the engineered tomatoes, but opinion was divided on whether they were an improvement.

The general lesson is that making genuine improvements to the flavour of tomatoes (or any other fruit) by genetic engineering, even where that is permitted, is too expensive and still too hit-and-miss to be a realistic option. Much more promising is using modern improvements in molecular biology to target conventional plant breeding, making it possible for the first time to transfer the flavour of heirloom varieties into modern cultivars, while still hanging on to the high yields and disease resistance of the modern variety. Perhaps the best news is that after many years in the wilderness, flavour is at last being taken seriously again as an objective in breeding fruit and vegetables.

INTERESTING THINGS ABOUT PLANTS

Colour change

When it comes to attracting pollinating insects, there are no prizes for being shy and retiring. The biggest and best floral displays attract the most visitors and ultimately produce the most seeds. One way plants can increase the size of the show is simply to make each individual flower work harder, by keeping flowers for longer before they fade. But although keeping flowers after they've been pollinated may attract more insects, there's a serious cost. Not only is keeping old flowers topped up with nectar wasteful, insects that visit such flowers are wasting their time as far as the plant is concerned. And if old flowers don't contain any nectar, visiting insects find no reward and are likely to give up in disgust.

The cunning way round this problem is to change the colour of the older flowers. Old flowers still contribute to the overall pollinator-attracting show, but insects soon learn that the altered colour means not to waste time visiting them. Probably the most familiar examples of this strategy in the average garden are the lungworts (*Pulmonaria* spp.), with flowers that start out red and become blue as they age. The whole lungwort family is prone to changing flower colour, sometimes dramatically; the wild changing forget-me-not (*Myosotis discolor*) opens yellow, before changing to the usual forget-me-not blue. It would be quite a spectacle if it weren't so tiny.

It's a clever idea, but such neat solutions always leave me with the same nagging question: if this is such a good idea, why don't all plants do it? Because obviously, they don't – most flowers just stay the same colour until they start to fade. The same question occurred to two Japanese biologists, who decided to investigate, in research published recently in the journal *Functional Ecology*.

The plants that attracted their attention were a pair of weigelas: *Weigela coraeensis* and *W. hortensis*. The flowers of the former open white but over about three days become red-purple, whereas the flowers of *W. hortensis* open pale pink and stay that way. Both are grown in gardens, although neither nearly as commonly as *W. florida*.

The first thing they discovered is that the colour-changing strategy certainly seems to work. In both plants flowers normally last about four days, but nectar production peaks in one-day-old flowers. In *Weigela coraeensis* bees strongly preferred to visit these young flowers, warned off the older flowers with little nectar by their red colour. But in *W. hortensis* bees were unable to tell young flowers (with lots of nectar) from older ones (with little nectar) and visited both about the same.

Differences between the plants emerged when the researchers experimentally enhanced pollination, by transferring pollen between flowers with a paintbrush, or prevented it altogether, by enclosing flowers in bee-proof bags. Essentially the two species have evolved different expectations of whether successful pollination will occur, and different ideas about what to do if it doesn't. So if pollination is prevented, *Weigela hortensis* doesn't do anything – flowers last about four days and then fade, as usual. On the other hand, flowers receiving extra pollen quickly fade, lasting only just over half as long. *Weigela coraeensis* behaves quite differently; flowers with extra pollen last about four days, as usual, but if pollination is prevented, it keeps on trying, so bagged flowers last for six days.

In other words, *W. hortensis* can quickly respond if pollination is successful, packing up its flowers and getting on with the important business of making seeds. *Weigela coraeensis*, on the other hand, seems scarcely able to believe its superior pollinator-attraction system isn't working, persisting with open flowers much longer if pollination is poor and, perhaps as a result, unable to shorten flower life if pollination happens quickly. One can imagine circumstances in which either strategy might pay more dividends, but it looks like for most plants, most of the time, the more pessimistic *W. hortensis* approach works out better, with only a minority of species adopting the colour-changing strategy.

Whatever the underlying biology, *Weigela coraeensis* is a strikingly attractive and unusual shrub that deserves to be more widely grown.

CSI plants

I wouldn't suggest for a moment that you are, but if – just for the sake of argument – you were planning the perfect murder, gardening would probably be the last thing on your mind. But the master criminal leaves nothing to chance, and botanical evidence is increasingly being used by police, so maybe you should spare a thought for plants.

Sometimes little real botany is involved, and plants simply add another element to traditional sleuthing. For example, in one recent case a man was found hanged from a tree. Death was clearly caused by asphyxia due to hanging, but was it murder or suicide? Traces of moss on the man's wrists matched that on the branches of the tree, presumably acquired while he was tying the rope to the branch, strongly suggesting suicide. Sometimes a bit more botany is required, as in a recent case in Taiwan. The body of a young woman was found at the edge of a road in Taipei. She had major impact injuries, but was she the victim of a hit-and-run driver, or did she fall from an adjacent block of flats? A sharp-eyed detective spotted a tiny fragment of plant material in her hair, and a search revealed a match to a plant in a window box a couple of floors up, proving that she fell to her death.

But some of the coolest botanical CSI, as in many areas of forensic science, is emerging from the use of DNA.

Sometimes this is because the plant itself is of criminal interest. For example, tiny traces of plant material, too small to use conventional chemical tests, can now confirm the presence of cannabis. American law enforcement agencies are also developing cannabis DNA databases, which not only allow them to tell exactly where a sample comes from, but can help to persuade people to plead guilty; for example a DNA match between marijuana sold by two different dealers can link them in a conspiracy case.

But sometimes the plant itself is innocent, even if the people it's linked to aren't. The iconic case took place in 1993, in the early days of DNA technology. A woman's body had been found in the Arizona desert at a site surrounded by palo verde trees, one of which showed damage from a recent collision. Examination of the suspect's pickup revealed two palo verde seed pods. Analysis of the DNA from the pods, the damaged tree, and 29 other trees confirmed beyond doubt that both seed pods came from the damaged tree, thus linking the vehicle to the murder site. In the subsequent trial, the seed pod data became the first molecular botanical evidence to be accepted by a court, and helped to convict the suspect of murder.

It doesn't always turn out like that. In a surprisingly similar case, the body of a pregnant woman was found buried in a shallow grave in a small wood in central Florida. Three large sand live oak trees (*Quercus geminata*) were found within a few yards, one with a canopy that spread over the grave. A suspect, linked to the crime by strong but only circumstantial evidence, was found to have leaves of *Q. geminata* in his car. Because the suspect denied ever being at the site, the leaves looked important. Which they were, but not in the way you might think; their DNA revealed they could *not* have come from any of the trees at the grave site.

Some botanical DNA evidence looks promising, but turns out not be. In a case in Spokane, Washington, DNA from honey locust (*Gleditsia triacanthos*) found at a crime scene was examined to see if it matched that from a tree in the suspect's garden. It did – but then it also matched the DNA from every other tree in town; honey locust is commonly propagated by grafting and *all* the local trees were genetically identical.

Finding a piece of a tree in a suspect's car is all very well, but not likely to happen all that often, and perhaps requires a more than usually careless criminal. But in a recent Dutch case, knotgrass (*Polygonum aviculare*) seeds were recovered from mud on a suspect's car. DNA from the seeds linked them conclusively to knotgrass plants growing by a track near to where a dead body had been dumped. It seems reasonable to expect that ubiquitous roadside weeds like knotgrass may often be useful in matching vehicles to crime scenes.

And all this time we thought weeds were useless. How mistaken we were.

. . . .✻. . . . .

Floral clocks

I must admit a partiality to evening primroses (*Oenothera* species), with their big, cheerful yellow flowers. Part of my liking is pure pragmatism; my garden is generally a bit dry, which is what evening primroses like, so I find them easy to grow. They also seem to be pretty slugproof. However, I would be the first to admit that the buttercup-yellow flowers of most members of the genus are just a bit common, an impression not helped by the fact that several have escaped into the wild. So I was pleased to run across an evening primrose in a Scottish garden that I didn't recognise, with lovely pale, primrose-yellow flowers, almost cream really. I helped myself to a few seeds – no great crime, since evening primrose seeds are tiny and produced in great numbers; a single plant could satisfy the evening primrose requirements of a small town – and they all germinated quite happily, so I was able to grow several large plants. Like most evening primroses, they do exactly what it says on the tin, i.e. flower in the evening. Each flower lasts less than 24 hours, and the previous evening's flowers slowly crumple and change colour during the following day, like pinky-red tissue paper, so that by about six o'clock the whole plant looks like something the cat brought in. Then, sometime between about seven and nine, a fresh batch unfurls and as dusk gradually deepens, the whole plant is transformed into a pillar of luminous, fragrant (in this species), ghostly yellow saucers. Few other garden plants are as exciting, as dynamic, as full of beans, as evening primroses.

It took me a while to figure out that my plant is *O. stricta*, which – unlike most species, which come from North America – hails from Chile, and is either the Chilean evening primrose or the fragrant evening primrose, according to who you believe. Oddly enough, the bog-standard species is as dandelion-yellow as the rest of them, and my version is a selection with paler flowers. Google reveals that such a plant is available under a variety of names, but most commonly as 'sulphurea'. Whatever it's called, it's highly recommended anyway, so worth looking out for; the RHS Plant Finder lists plenty of suppliers. Its only downside is that like most evening primroses, it's a biennial, so you have to start again from seed every year, although if you're lucky it will self-seed – it does in my garden.

Evening primrose's timekeeping started me thinking about floral clocks. And no, I don't mean the sort involving a carpet of begonias and houseleeks, two big hands and the words 'Welcome to Eastbourne', or whatever. No, I was thinking more about the old idea of telling the time by the opening and closing of flowers, an idea so old in fact that it certainly predates clocks, at least in the modern sense. Some of the most evocative names of our native wildflowers refer to their role as timekeepers, and both my favourites are 'early-closers'. Scarlet pimpernel (*Anagallis arvensis*) is a nice enough name, but even better is old man's weathervane, or poor man's weatherglass. Scarlet pimpernel flowers open in the morning and close about 2.00pm, but its reliability depends a lot on the weather; if it's dull or wet, the flowers close earlier, or never open at all. Much more reliable, in my experience, is goat's beard (*Tragopogon pratensis*) or Jack-go-to-bed-at-noon, whose large dandelion-like flowers really do close fairly promptly around lunchtime, rain or shine.

It's a short step from such informal names to the idea of constructing a clock that allows you to tell the time by the opening and closing of flowers. This is a notion with a long pedigree, one of the most famous examples being the clock ('*Horologium florae*') designed by Linnaeus himself, the inventor of our modern system of Latin plant names. There's no evidence that Linnaeus ever actually planted his clock, but if he had – and if it had worked as planned – observing the opening and closing of the flowers should have enabled you to tell the time at least to the nearest hour. I don't personally recommend Linnaeus's clock, for at least two reasons. First, most of the 45 plants listed are wildflowers, or even weeds, and an alarming proportion are vaguely dandelion-like (and very similar) members of the daisy family. In other words, however good it is at telling the time, it's unlikely to draw many gasps of admiration for its aesthetic appeal. Second, flowering behaviour depends a lot on climate and latitude, and Linnaeus's clock was designed to work in Uppsala in Sweden, not in Britain.

Oddly enough, Linnaeus's clock doesn't use my favourite floral timepiece, evening primrose, even though one or two species had been in cultivation in Europe for at least a century by the time he was writing. In fact it seems Linnaeus couldn't think of any plant with reliable evening-opening flowers, and the best he could do for this time of day was the day-lily *Hemerocallis lilio-asphodelus*, whose flowers are closing about the time evening primrose is opening. Linnaeus's clock does use goat's beard, but for its *opening* rather than closing time, which he claims is 3.00am, a time that – for reasons that I hope are obvious – I cannot confirm. But knowing that Linnaeus felt it worthwhile to include 3.00am in his clock does at least suggest how he managed to get through such a prodigious amount of work in his lifetime, including naming every species known at the time; it looks like he was an early riser.

. . . . ✳ . . . .

Nicotiana: *how not to poison your pollinators*

Nicotiana is a popular enough genus in the garden, but maybe it would be even more popular if gardeners knew how much interesting biology lurks behind those beautiful flowers. Like several other popular garden flowers, nicotianas have evolved very different flowers to suit different pollinators. Pale-coloured flowers, often with long petal tubes and a strong scent, are pollinated by various hawkmoths. But nicotianas are from the warmer parts of America, and many species have evolved to be pollinated by hummingbirds. These species typically have red flowers with a shorter tube, and no scent. Similar variation can be seen in honeysuckles and columbines, each with red-flowered species (pollinated by hummingbirds) and pale-flowered species (pollinated by moths). Our native columbine, with blue flowers, is a bee specialist.

Something else we all know about tobacco is that like the rest of the Solanaceae family, it often contains quite large quantities of toxic alkaloids; in *Nicotiana*, of course, mostly nicotine. *Nicotiana rustica* was Raleigh's original tobacco, but it contains dangerously high levels of nicotine, so was quite quickly superseded by the milder *N. tabacum*. Both will still kill you, of course, it just takes a bit longer with *N. tabacum*. Neither of these species is widely grown in British gardens, not least because *N. rustica* is not very attractive and *N. tabacum* is enormous.

Interestingly, according to new research in the journal *Ecology Letters*, nicotine and pollination in *Nicotiana* are inextricably linked. The plants manufacture nicotine in their roots, from where it is transported to the rest of the plant. Its function is to deter the animals, especially various caterpillars, that would otherwise like to eat the rather soft and tasty leaves (sadly, it doesn't seem to work too well against slugs). But this defence against insects presents *Nicotiana* with something of a predicament, because it doesn't seem to be very good at keeping the nicotine out of its nectar, or at least not completely. Thus, although *Nicotiana* nectar does contain less nicotine than the rest of the plant, the two levels are still related; species with lots of nicotine in their leaves also have relatively high levels in their nectar – high enough to deter most pollinators.

Some species have decided to tolerate this limitation to their defensive armoury and have relatively low levels of nicotine. But others have really gone to town on the nicotine, avoiding the risk of poisoning their pollinators by evolving self-pollination. No longer reliant on pollinators, such species can have as much nicotine in their leaves as they like – in practice, about fifteen times more than the species that still depend on pollinators. *Nicotiana rustica*, whose leaves can be up to 9 per cent nicotine, has gone down this route.

Does any of this influence which *Nicotiana* species deserve a space in your garden? Not really; you should obviously grow what you like. But gardeners who take an interest in their local pollinators should grow species that are (a) moth-pollinated and (b) unlikely to poison their insect visitors. Two lovely plants that satisfy both criteria, and are widely available, are *N. sylvestris* and *N. alata*, both with the added bonus of a gorgeous scent (*N. alata* is not called jasmine tobacco for nothing). *Nicotiana sylvestris* is the one to go for if you want a plant that makes a real statement, growing six feet or more tall, with leaves to match. Slightly less widely grown, but reckoned by some to have the best scent of all, is *N. noctiflora*. Becoming very fashionable is *N. mutabilis*, a new species from Brazil first described only ten years ago. Its flowers, as the name suggests, gradually change colour, starting out creamy white and becoming deep pink, but it's a hummingbird species, so it has little or no scent and will not attract moths.

The final thing to remember about nicotianas is that although many are perennials, all are rather tender and best grown as half-hardy annuals in British gardens.

. . . . ❋ . . . .

How plants flower in winter

At a time of year when there's often little else to be cheerful about, I'm sure we're all grateful for plants that flower in winter. But around this time of year, many of you probably find yourselves wondering why plants bother (they don't do it just for our enjoyment). There are two serious problems: pollinators are scarce, and low temperatures make it difficult for the pollen to germinate or the young seed to grow. Over the years, botanists have discovered that plants have figured out at least two ways round this problem. One simple solution is for the flower itself to generate heat, and here the arums are the kings: eastern skunk cabbage (*Symplocarpus foetidus*) can keep its flowers above 15°C when air temperature is −15°C and can often be seen melting the snow around the plants. In fact skunk cabbage generates more heat than almost anything else on the planet, gram for gram, more even than a hummingbird working flat out.

From a gardener's perspective, eastern skunk cabbage is really only a curiosity – it's certainly no oil painting, and perhaps worth growing only for those who like to grow things they can be pretty sure no one else has (do not confuse with *western* skunk cabbage, which *is* widely grown in gardens). To add to its appearance, it doesn't smell very nice either (it's not called skunk cabbage for nothing), and not surprisingly, there are few British suppliers. One curious fact is that all that starch needed to generate the heat makes skunk cabbage an attractive food, and in its native North America it is enthusiastically consumed by bears emerging from hibernation.

Generating your own heat burns a lot of starch, and a cheaper solution (although one that works only in an open site) is flowers that focus and trap the sun's heat, often accompanied by sun-tracking behaviour. The parabolic flowers of mountain avens (*Dryas octopetala*) and Arctic poppy (*Papaver radicatum*) both track the sun and can get up to 10°C above ambient on a still, sunny day. A variation on this theme is 'microgreenhouse' flowers that allow heat to enter through translucent petals and then trap this heat within closed flowers; crocuses are good at this. Experiments have shown that since bees don't enjoy being frozen stiff any more than we do, all these heating options encourage pollinators to visit.

Until recently, we thought solar heating and internally generated heat exhausted the options, but new research shows there's a third way. Botanists in Spain were perplexed to discover that *Helleborus foetidus* (stinking hellebore) flowers can get up to 6°C above ambient, but have no internal heat source and grow in shade where solar heating is unavailable. How do they do this? The rather surprising answer turns out to be yeast, in fact a rather specific yeast called *Metschnikowia reukaufii*. The yeast is capable of rapid fermentation of the sugars in nectar, generating considerable heat in the process. The researchers were able to show that preventing yeasts from colonising young flowers stopped them warming up, and experimentally adding yeast restored that ability; in the wild, yeast cells are moved around by pollinating bumblebees, so almost all flowers contain yeast. Although this rather remarkable strategy was discovered only recently, it's already clear that it may be common among early-flowering plants of shady habitats. No one has yet done the temperature measurements, but primroses (among others) contain precisely the same yeast, and probably warm up in exactly the same way.

But hellebores are treading on thin ice here – although warmer flowers attract more bees, rapidly respiring yeast can remove almost all the sugar in the nectar, thus discouraging visits by pollinators. It's possible that bees adjust their foraging accordingly, going for sweeter (but cooler) flowers on warm days and warmer (but less sugary) flowers when it's a bit parky. And – potentially – there's another problem, for the bees at least, since all that fermented sugar is turned into alcohol. The flowers of one Malaysian palm contain yeasts that turn nectar into up to 3.8 per cent alcohol, and the tree-shrews that pollinate the palm spend their lives in a permanent state of inebriation. But so far, the effect of binge drinking on bumblebees has yet to attract the attention of researchers.

. . . . ❄ . . . .

The rat-race to get out of the shade

Take a look out of the window at the plants in your garden. Look peaceful, don't they? It's difficult to appreciate how nervous they really are, in fact deeply worried. And what are they worried about? Each other.

Plants need light, and being deprived of light means fairly rapid death. Almost the worst thing that can happen to a plant is to be overtopped by a neighbouring plant, and thus shaded and deprived of light, so plants that are used to plenty of light make strenuous efforts to make sure this doesn't happen. In fact a sure sign that plants such as aspidistras are genuinely shade-tolerant is that in response to shade, they do – nothing. In contrast, plants that need lots of light respond very quickly to a shortage, growing as fast as they can towards the nearest available light, often becoming pale and spindly ('etiolated') as they do so.

But how do plants know that shade is about to become a problem? If they wait until shade really *is* a problem, it may be too late, because that means a competitor is already taller than they are. So plants have evolved to respond not to the quantity of light, but to its quality. Plants do not use the whole visible spectrum for photosynthesis, they mainly use red light, which is why they look green (if you take the red out of daylight, you are mostly left with green). However, the light just along the spectrum from red, but not quite infra-red, known as *far-red*, is not used at all. Ordinary sunlight contains lots of red, but light reflected from leaves contains little red and thus relatively more far-red light, so the red/far-red ratio acts as a kind of early-warning system for the detection of other plants. To make use of this property, all plants contain a chemical that is switched between two different forms by red and far-red light.

Thus plants are able to detect the presence of other plants nearby, long before they cast any serious shade, by measuring the spectrum of the light reflected from their leaves. In one classic experiment, purslane seedlings grew away from a strip of green plastic only 2 cm high, far too small to cause any real shade, because the light reflected from it was low in red. During evolution, light with the red taken out has proved to be such a good guide to trouble ahead that purslane now needs 'ordinary' shade 50 times deeper to balance the repellent effect of 'green' shade.

But light can't always be used to spot an encroaching neighbour. Before they flower, rosettes of the common garden weed thale cress are basically flat (too flat to cast any shade or affect the red/far-red ratio), so what happens when they meet? New research in the journal *PNAS* shows that here touch is crucial. When the leaf edges touch they begin to grow up, away from the soil, in an effort to shade their neighbour. Touching any obstruction makes the leaves do this (clear plastic will do), and only the touching leaves grow upwards – the rest of the plant stays flat.

But although plants like to keep up with their neighbours, they don't necessarily want to grow much taller, because plants that stick up too far risk losing too much water or being damaged by wind. In one cunning experiment, reported in the journal *New Phytologist*, pots containing the common weed fat hen were arranged in a block. If a pot was lowered below the general level, the plant in it grew faster, but if it was raised up, it slowed down, so after a while the tops of all the plants ended up at more or less the same level. Further cunning experiments showed that the fat hen plants use light quality *and* touch to keep tabs on their neighbours, and showed this normal 'converging' behaviour only if they could use both kinds of information.

So the plants in your garden may not look like they're doing much, but they're constantly monitoring their place in the horticultural rat-race, and adjusting their behaviour to keep up with the Joneses.

· · · · · · ·❋· · · · · · · ·

The secret life of spores

What's the most annoying plant in your garden? Hairy bittercress? Ground elder? Chances are, if you're unfortunate enough to have it, it's horsetail – the plant that outlived the dinosaurs, and is quite likely to outlive you too. So you can imagine it's a challenge to find anything to like about horsetail, still less to admire, but here goes.

Horsetails, like ferns, are primitive plants that reproduce by spores. Spores are tiny and very light, so once they get airborne, they can travel vast distances on the wind. But it's that initial step that's the problem. Some kind of launch mechanism is required, a problem that ferns and horsetails have solved in completely different ways.

Spores are contained in sporangia, and the fern sporangium is a miniature marvel of engineering. A strip of cells along one side have thickened radial and inner walls, and as the sporangium loses water the cells shrink, simultaneously breaking the sporangium open and bending it backwards. When the strain becomes too great, a bubble of air comes out of solution in each cell (*cavitation*), releasing the tension and allowing the sporangium to snap back to its original shape, flinging the spores out at up to 10 metres per second. This briefly exposes the spores to g-forces that would squash you or me like a pancake, but fortunately spores are much tougher than people. The whole operation resembles the action of a medieval siege catapult.

In stark contrast to the elegant ballistic machinery of ferns, horsetail sporangia don't do anything; they're just bags of spores. The magic lies in the spores themselves, each of which has four ribbon-like structures attached called elaters.

Each elater has a tough, waterproof side and a more elastic, hygroscopic side that expands and contracts as it absorbs and loses water. The result is that when the spore is wet, the elaters are tightly coiled around the spore, but as the spore dries they unfurl, until a dry spore looks like a spider with half its legs missing. This coiling and uncoiling helps the spores to spill out of the sporangium, and once on the ground, allows them to 'walk' around (although they don't get very far, and always run the risk of walking around in circles and ending up back where they started).

But they have a secret weapon, only recently discovered by French researchers and reported in the journal *Proceedings of the Royal Society*. If spores are really wet, the elaters can become tangled up. As the spore dries they at first remain tangled but then abruptly straighten, releasing their energy like the sudden uncoiling of a spring, propelling the spore up to 1 cm into the air at up to 1 metre per second. That may not seem like much, but for an object less than 0.005 cm across, it's an immense distance, like a human leaping over the Shard, with a few feet to spare.

That's more than enough to boost the spore up into the breeze, the first step on its way to who knows where (likely as not some other poor sod's garden). It's also, the researchers suggest, likely to inspire the design of a whole new class of self-propelled objects, powered only by alternating sun and rain. Something to think about while you're trying to dig the damn things up, or applying yet another dose of glyphosate.

········✳········

A temperate Tarzan?

It's hard to imagine a temperate – as opposed to tropical – Tarzan. For one thing, it's just too damn cold. Swinging through the trees in a loincloth is all very well, but doing the same in an overcoat, gloves and woolly hat is clearly silly. But there's another problem, which is the shortage in temperate woodland of things to swing *from*. The favoured Tarzan locomotion aid is a handy liana, but there simply aren't many of those around outside the tropics. In tropical forest, around a quarter of all woody plants are lianas, but in temperate forests the proportion is around 10 per cent or even less. Given that that's only 10 per cent of a much smaller number of plants anyway, that's not many lianas.

Gardeners know this only too well. We grow a couple of wisterias, a few honeysuckles, and an awful lot of clematis, but as soon as we want to grow something a bit different, it often turns out to be a bit tender: think *Trachelospermum, Eccremocarpus, Bougainvillea, Passiflora, Lapageria* and so on. So why is that? I'll come to that in a minute, but first, why are lianas so successful anyway, especially in the tropics?

For plants, the big advantage of climbing is not having to waste resources on being self-supporting, i.e. on lots of wood. In trees, the water-conducting cells (xylem) have to do two jobs: act as a pipe for water and help to hold the tree up. In lianas, they can specialise completely on transport, which means they can be wider, which in turn makes them much more efficient. So lianas can effortlessly transport water to great heights, despite having much narrower stems than trees.

So much for the tropics, but how well does this work in colder climates? A popular theory is that wide xylem cells are susceptible to embolism in winter; that is, air comes out of solution when the water in the xylem freezes and then doesn't re-dissolve when the ice melts, leaving an air bubble in the pipe. And plants' plumbing, just like yours, doesn't work if it gets air in it, which means the main competitive advantage of lianas disappears in climates with freezing winter temperatures. This is one reason conifers are so successful in cold climates – they have primitive xylem cells called tracheids that are very narrow, which makes them highly resistant to freezing embolism.

It's a good theory, but like many good theories it's rarely been tested, which makes a recent paper in the journal *Functional Ecology* from a couple of Chilean botanists so interesting. They looked at a collection of trees and lianas from evergreen temperate rainforest in Chile, where the climate is mild and wet, but still cold enough to freeze in winter. Several of the trees will be well-known to gardeners, especially *Eucryphia cordifolia*, one of the parents of the popular hybrid cultivar 'Nymansay'. Other familiar species, especially to those who garden in warmer parts of the UK, included the trees *Gevuina avellana* (Chilean hazel) and *Luma apiculata* (Chilean myrtle) and the beautiful red-flowered climber *Berberidopsis corallina*.

Their results were completely consistent with the freezing embolism theory. The lianas did indeed have xylem cells that were wider and much more efficient than those of the trees. But after exposure to freezing winter temperatures, the climbers lost a much higher fraction of their water-conducting ability than the trees. Some of the climbers could repair the damage by actively pumping water back into the xylem from the roots, but this takes a lot of energy, and in any case it works only if the plant isn't very tall.

So quite apart from ordinary frost damage to leaves and shoots, the vascular plumbing of lianas from warmer climates just doesn't work in a climate with sub-zero winter temperatures. Nor is there any way round the problem – lagging, I fear, is not the answer.

. . . .✳. . . . .

Variegation

Most gardeners probably have room for two or three variegated plants, although as a class they've never really been fashionable. But maybe they would be if people realised how much fascinating biology (and physics) there is going on beneath the surface.

The first thing you need to know is that variegation is not one but two quite distinct things. The simplest, and probably the commonest, is pigment variegation, where the non-green parts of the leaf simply lack chlorophyll. Sometimes these parts have no pigments at all and look white, but more often there are other pigments present, so they look cream or yellow. The lack of pigment is a mutation, but the precise pattern depends on where this mutation occurs. In the growing point of the stem (the 'meristem') the outer layer of cells gives rise to the surface and edges of the leaf, so a mutation here gives you a leaf with a green centre and white or yellow edges. The cells in the core of the meristem make up the rest of the leaf, so a mutation here means a green edge and a white or yellow centre. Technically, plants that are made up of two genetically different kinds of cells are known as chimeras after the Chimera of Greek mythology, which was part lion, part snake, part goat. And fire-breathing too, so basically pretty scary. Plant chimeras are much less frightening, and include many popular garden plants, e.g. variegated ivies, hollies, hostas, dogwoods, daphnes, *Elaeagnus* and many others. *Euonymus japonicus* illustrates the two patterns of variegation particularly well, since it exists in both 'mirror-image' forms: green with a white or (yellow) margin, and white (or yellow) with a green margin.

Completely different is structural variegation, in which pigments are not involved at all. Here there is an air-filled gap between the outer epidermis of the leaf and the chlorophyll-containing cells beneath. Structural variegation exploits a phenomenon known as *total internal reflection*, which happens when light passes from a dense medium (with a high refractive index) to a less dense one (with a lower refractive index). If light hits this boundary at greater than the critical angle (in this case 44°), it is completely reflected back into the denser medium. Swimmers among you can experience this by opening your eyes just under the water surface, when you will see that the water surface looks like a mirror. Optical fibres wouldn't work without total internal reflection.

In the case of leaves, light meeting the boundary between the epidermis and the air gap at greater than the critical angle is reflected back out of the upper surface of the leaf, resulting in a characteristic silvery variegation. Many garden plants have this kind of variegation (*Pulmonaria* is a nice example), but the kings of structural variegation are probably the begonias. Many *Begonia* species have structural variegation, and indeed the phenomenon was first described in the 1950s in *B.* × *argenteo-guttata* and *B. rex*, both of which have given rise to many of today's ornamental variegated cultivars.

One curiosity is *B. chlorosticta*, which has stunningly beautiful dark green leaves with a light green margin and spots. It has the same structural variegation as all the other begonias, so why isn't it just green and silver like them? The answer, according to recent research by a team from Taiwan and published in the journal *Annals of Botany*, is the red pigment in the lower epidermis of the leaves of this species. Apparently you can reproduce the same effect in a normal green-and-silver begonia by painting the lower surface with red nail varnish, although this is not a recommended horticultural technique.

For the gardener, there are big practical differences between the two sorts of variegation. Because the parts of leaves without chlorophyll cannot photosynthesise, shoots with pigment variegation are always less vigorous than green ones. The mutation is often unstable, so you need to be on the lookout for green ('reverted') shoots and remove them before they take over. Shoots on my variegated *Euonymus japonicus* revert all the time. But in leaves with structural variegation reversion is more or less impossible, and it wouldn't matter anyway, since variegated leaves work just as well as green ones. Pigment variegation is also confined to the bits of the plant that are actually variegated, so should come true from a shoot cutting, but probably not from a root cutting and certainly not from seed. Structural variegation, on the other hand, is just something the plant does, so will come true from any kind of cutting, or from seed.

. . . . ❋ . . . .

The Swiss cheese plant: why holes are an advantage

If you own a Swiss cheese plant (*Monstera deliciosa*), do you ever wonder why it has leaves with holes in, and whether there are other plants that do the same? The latter question is much the simpler: the answer is very few indeed, mostly just a few other species of *Monstera*. The former question didn't have a plausible answer at all until recently, but Chris Muir of Indiana University has put us all out of our misery, in a paper published in the journal *American Naturalist*. Unfortunately, the answer is not exactly simple, and before we proceed it might be as well, like Jeeves, to make sure the old brain is on tip-top form by eating plenty of fish.

Swiss cheese plants are climbers that grow in the understorey of tropical American forests and are technically *hemiepiphytes*. That is, they start off in the ground like any normal plant. They then grow, unusually, *away* from the light, which helps them to find the nearest tree trunk, up which they scramble. Later they produce aerial roots and may ultimately lose all connection with the ground, but in the corner of your office or living room, they generally stay firmly rooted in soil.

It's mostly pretty dark where Swiss cheese plants grow, so they depend a lot on sunflecks, occasional shafts of sunlight that penetrate the dense tree canopy. Sunflecks are so very much brighter than the prevailing gloom that even though they are rare and unpredictable, they may account for more than half of the cheese plant's total photosynthesis. For a Swiss cheese plant, making good use of sunflecks is a matter of life and death. So why are leaves with holes in them better at this?

First, it's obvious that for a given amount of actual leaf, a leaf with holes can be bigger than an entire leaf, i.e. one without holes. Imagine, for example, a really enormous (and quite unrealistic) cheese plant leaf, say the size of a sheet. Such a leaf would be much more hole than leaf, but its size means it would encounter sunflecks all the time, even though most of them would go straight through one of the many holes. An entire leaf with the same area of actual leaf would meet a sunfleck only rarely, but would be able to use all those it did encounter. Thus the big, hole-filled leaf would experience more or less the same, low but steady amount of sunfleck every day, while the much smaller entire leaf would experience only an occasional bonanza.

Some simple maths (trust me) shows that over the long term, both leaves would encounter exactly the same total amount of sunfleck. So why is one better than the other? Well, as far as natural selection is concerned, what matters is not just the average performance of the two leaves (which, as we've seen, is the same), but how variable they are – and variability is bad. Imagine the leaf is an investor, acquiring a dividend (in this case carbon via photosynthesis) and re-investing that dividend to acquire more carbon. As your financial advisor will tell you, a risky investment, which may deliver high returns but might also do very poorly, is not as good as one that delivers a lower but reliable return. The reason is that over the long term, occasional bad years depress yield more than occasional good ones increase it.

To illustrate this, imagine you invest a sum for three years and get a return of 10 per cent in each year (I know, chance would be a fine thing, but bear with me). How does that compare to 5 per cent in year one, 10 per cent in year two, and 15 per cent in year three? Since the average of 5, 10 and 15 is 10, surely they are the same? No they're not – the variable rate delivers an average return of only 9.92 per cent per year over the three years. Not a lot less than 10 per cent, but less nevertheless, and the more variable things get, the worse the return; 1, 10 and 19 per cent (still with an average of 10 per cent) delivers only 9.75 per cent.

This is a Big Idea in evolutionary biology, and explains why evolutionary changes that reduce variability tend to get selected, even if they don't change average performance. So Aesop was right all along – slow and steady wins the race. Or to put it another way, if you understand your Swiss cheese plant, you're halfway to understanding most things.

. . . . . . ··✳··· . . . . . .

England and Scotland – going their separate ways?

So, the Scots (or at least 55 per cent of them) have decided to stick with the Union.* But such a merely political decision cannot influence biological reality, which is that from a botanical perspective, England and Scotland are a long way down the road to being separate countries.

How do I know this? Because the first-ever Red List for English plants was launched at Kew Gardens last week. Red Lists exist for many different groups of animals and plants,

* This was published just after the Scottish independence referendum.

in many different countries, and use established criteria to identify those species that are threatened by serious decline, or even extinction. There are British Red Lists for everything from fungi to butterflies, and the British Red List for plants was published in 2005. A Red List for Wales followed in 2008, but this is the first list for England. Preparation of the list was funded by English Nature, but the raw data come from the BSBI's (Botanical Society of Britain and Ireland) army of volunteer plant counters and recorders.

There are several criteria for being listed, but the commonest one is decline since 1930. Species in the highest 'critically endangered' category have declined by 80 per cent or more over that time. One or two of these plants are well known: lady's slipper orchid, for example, partly on account of its spectacular beauty, and partly because of the strenuous efforts made to conserve it. But it's a fair bet that you've never heard of the great majority of the most threatened plants. You never knew *Diphasiastrum complanatum* (Issler's clubmoss, down to a single site) or *Damasonianum alisma* (starfruit, barely hanging on) were here in the first place, so you're unlikely to notice they've gone.

But to me, the most startling news is not about these very rare plants, many of which were never particularly common. It's what the list tells us about the decline of plants that I still think of as common, even very common. Between the three 'threatened' categories and 'no need to worry' (technically, 'least concern'), we find 'near threatened' plants. These are species that haven't declined enough to qualify as threatened, but show a worrying downward trend; the implication being that if things carry on as they are, they will be in trouble before long. In this camp we find, among many others, devil's bit scabious and field scabious, beautiful (and previously common) wild plants that I grow in my garden. But most alarmingly, and I still can't believe I'm writing this: heather. No, that's not a misprint, I really mean heather, ling, *Calluna vulgaris*.

I can walk to places in the Peak District where I can see almost nothing but heather as far as the eye can see. How can such a plant be 'near threatened'? The answer is that the Peak District is a southern outpost of upland Britain, where heather is indeed one of the commonest plants around. So at the UK scale (including Scotland), or in Wales, heather is still very common, as it always has been. In lowland Britain (i.e. in England), heather used to be fairly common too, but pressure from urbanisation, pollution, the decline of traditional land management and intensive farming means it's declined dramatically.

Some plants are faring even worse. *Parnassia palustris*, with a 39 per cent decline, is actually threatened in England, but in no trouble at all once you include Scotland and Wales. Grass of Parnassus, a lovely name for a lovely plant, is my candidate for the most delicately beautiful plant in our native flora, and not grown in gardens nearly as widely as it ought to be (only one supplier in the RHS Plant Finder). It's still a plant I expect to see on a walk in the limestone dales of the Peak District, where it's doing OK, thriving even, but south of here – apart from a few beleaguered outposts – it's a goner.

It looks like Ed Miliband isn't the only one dependent on Scotland for his continued survival* – many of our native plants are too.

. . . .✳ . . . .

Dioecious imports

Most plants are hermaphrodite, even if some of them (hazel, for example) keep their male and female flowers apart. But some plants are *dioecious*, i.e. they have separate sexes. Some of our most familiar wild plants, such as nettle and red campion, are dioecious, and if your holly never has any berries, that's probably because it's a male.

An interesting situation arises when only one sex of an alien dioecious plant is imported into the UK. This again involves some very familiar plants; perhaps none more so than Japanese knotweed, where all the plants in

* Clearly this was written before the 2015 general election.

Britain belong to the same female clone. Thus our Japanese knotweed is incapable of setting seed, although it does occasionally do so by crossing with other (alien) species of knotweed. This means that apart from bits of rhizome being washed down rivers, it can get around only by being moved in contaminated soil. The frequency with which it does this is a sign of just what a careless bunch we are.

Pampas grass (*Cortaderia selloana*) is more complicated. In its native Argentina, about half the plants are hermaphrodite and about half are female, but the hermaphrodite plants apparently don't put much effort into producing seeds. In other words, hermaphrodites are effectively male and thus pampas grass is effectively dioecious. According to a short article in *BSBI News* a few years ago from James Armitage at RHS Wisley, female and hermaphrodite plants look rather different, and the flowering plumes of female plants are generally reckoned to be more attractive. Certainly most of the available cultivars are female, as are the three that have the RHS Award of Garden Merit.

Pampas grass is highly invasive in some other parts of the world, but Armitage reckons that this preference for females by British gardeners may have slowed down its escape into the wild in Britain; for a long time there weren't enough males to allow all those suburban females to produce many seeds. But once a few self-sown plants did appear, some of these turned out to be male, which allowed the females to produce more seeds, some of which were male … and so on. Certainly pampas grass made a slow start in the wild in Britain; despite being grown here since 1848, it was recorded in only 21 hectads (10 × 10 km squares) up to 1986, but is now recorded in 425.

According to an article in a more recent *BSBI News*, another plant we're going to see a lot more of is winter heliotrope (*Petasites fragrans*), another garden escape that has made itself a bit too much at home. With its large, kidney-shaped leaves and heads of vanilla-scented flowers in winter, winter heliotrope is already a familiar sight along many a road verge. But our plants are all male so, like Japanese knotweed, it has so far had to rely entirely on bits of plant being moved around.

But sharp-eyed botanist Arthur Hoare has now found the female plant growing both in and around Borde Hill Garden in West Sussex. No one knows how it comes to be there, but the head gardener confirms that it's already a bit of a problem in the garden. An inability to produce seeds has hardly held back the male plant in the wild in Britain, where it is already in over 2,000 hectads, but free for the first time in 200 years to enjoy the delights of some female company, this Mediterranean native may manage to do even better in future.

. . . .❋. . . . .

Tall or short, and not much in between

Plenty of people have written entire books about trees, and even more have done the same for shrubs. Most of my gardening books have separate sections for trees and shrubs. So what is the difference between a tree and a shrub? One difference, of course, is that trees typically have a single main trunk, while shrubs often have multiple stems, but in truth this difference (which isn't universal anyway) is merely a means to an end. And that end is height – trees are taller than shrubs.

But, despite trees and shrubs occupying different parts of books, or often different books, I had somehow always assumed that when it came to height, woody plants were a bit like people, i.e. that variation in height was a smooth, bell-shaped curve. So that although we can talk about short or tall people, or short or tall woody plants (i.e. shrubs and trees), these are merely arbitrary chunks of a continuous distribution of height.

But a new analysis of a huge global plant database, reported in the journal *Trends in Ecology & Evolution*, shows that it's not like that. The distribution of height in woody plants clearly has two peaks, with a distinct trough between them. One peak has an average height of 26 metres, the other a height of 2.8 metres. In other words, trees and shrubs are not just arbitrary labels, a consequence of the overpowering human desire to classify and name anything and everything. They really exist.

The question, of course, is why? Why do most woody plants want to be tall, or short, but apparently not somewhere in between – specifically, why is about 8–10 metres high so unpopular? The authors of the report make two points.

The first is the rather obvious one that the world's natural vegetation is divided rather sharply into two very broad types: those that are dominated by trees and those that aren't. In the parts where it's too dry, too cold, too windy or burns too often for trees, woody plants don't have to grow tall to compete for light, so they don't. Here, all they have to do is beat the herbaceous competition, which is easy – the same database shows that while herbaceous (non-woody) plants vary a lot, they average only around 1 metre in height.

In woodland, woody plants have to compete with each other for light, and the only way to do that is to grow tall. Of course, that doesn't in itself explain why trees have to be so much taller than shrubs. Put simply, trees don't 'need' to be so tall. If an average tree is 26 metres tall, then the canopy of leaves is sitting on top of at least 20 metres of fairly useless wood, but it would work just as well (and still easily be tall enough to beat the shrubby competition) if the trunk were only, say, 10 metres tall.

Trees are taller than they 'need' to be because they are the victims of a classic prisoner's dilemma (a prisoner's dilemma is where the behaviour – or possible behaviour – of others forces you to do something you'd probably be better off not doing). Essentially if all trees could agree to be a bit shorter, they would all be better off (for example, they would be less likely to fall over in high winds). But not only is there no way for trees to agree on such a policy, it wouldn't help if there were. Even people, who are capable (theoretically anyway) of coming to rational agreements, often find themselves stuck in a prisoner's dilemma, because we don't trust each other.

So trees are forced to play the dangerous game of being taller than they would like – so tall in fact that the tallest trees are limited only by the laws of physics. Shrubs, which aren't playing the same game at all, can be much smaller. The woody plants (treelets? trubs?) between these two extremes have the worst of both worlds: they're not tall enough where being tall is important, and too tall where it isn't. Which is why there aren't very many.

PRACTICAL
GARDENING

Compost – getting the temperature right

Making your own compost turns waste into a valuable material that supplies nutrients, improves soil structure and suppresses weeds. So most of us do it and, if they're being honest, even those who don't do it know they should.

But there has always been a good degree of (justifiable) paranoia about what can safely go on the compost heap. Essentially it's a question of temperature – a hot compost heap kills most things, but a cool one doesn't. Sometimes there are ways round this. Roots and rhizomes of perennial weeds will survive in a cool compost heap, but you can always kill them first. One way to do this, and to my mind the most satisfying, is to beat them to a pulp with a hammer, but just leaving them somewhere dry until thoroughly shrivelled works just as well in the end. But there is no such easy solution for weed seeds, and those that survive for long periods in soil (which is most of them, sadly) will do exactly the same in a cool compost heap.

Plant pests and diseases have always been problematical too, especially with the arrival of a whole raft of new killers that we need to worry about – sudden oak death (*Phytophthora ramorum*) and ash dieback (*Chalara fraxinea*), for example. Again, temperature is the key, so how hot does a heap need to be? Research shows that pests and diseases vary in their temperature tolerance, but that 50°C for at least seven days is enough to see off *Phytophthora* (including potato blight), clubroot, nematodes, the various organisms that cause damping-off, plus larvae of carrot, onion and narcissus flies. But you need a really hot compost heap to kill viruses, perhaps because they're hardly alive in the first place.

So much for the good news. How likely is your compost heap to attain 50°C for seven days? Not very likely is the answer. The crucial difficulty, for the average gardener, is size. Paul Alexander, the Royal Horticultural Society's compost wizard, compared open heaps, small plastic bins (like the ones often supplied by local authorities) and traditional wooden bins, all filled with a 50/50 mixture of shredded woody and soft green waste collected from the RHS garden at Wisley. There were subtle differences between bin types, with the wooden bin being slightly warmer, although it's hard to say whether this was because it was rather larger or because wood is a better insulator. Turning helped too, with bins turned once a month being slightly warmer than those left unturned. But the bottom line is that none of the bins got more than a few degrees above air temperature, and certainly none got anywhere near 50°C. The raw material was clearly fine, because a giant 70 cubic metre heap of the same stuff stayed above 40°C, and most of the time above 50°C, for a whole year.

The small compost heaps, typical of the size found in the average garden, stayed cold because they have too much surface area relative to their volume. In order to heat up reliably, a compost heap almost certainly needs to be significantly bigger than 1 cubic metre. It also needs to be filled up pretty quickly, since a heap filled slowly over a few weeks (the normal garden pattern) stands even less chance of becoming hot. A final problem to bear in mind is that even a hot compost heap will be much cooler at the surface, the edges and especially (in a square bin) the corners, so the heap needs to be turned carefully so that these outer parts end up in the middle. All this makes proper 'hot' composting hard work in the average-sized garden.

What is the gardener to do? All the owner of a normal, cool compost heap can hope to do is try to stop diseases and weed seeds getting into the heap in the first place. The determined compost cooker needs a bin that is specially designed to keep the heat in. The recently introduced HOTBIN® is designed to do just that, essentially by being heavily insulated. I haven't tried a HOTBIN myself, but everything I hear (from *Which?*, for example) suggests they work a treat.

. . . . ❋ . . . .

Conifers and soil pH

I'm sometimes asked if conifers can acidify the soil underneath them. The short answer is yes, but as usual the long answer is not quite so simple. Note first of all that it's a waste of time just to wander out into the countryside and start measuring soil pH under different trees, because trees naturally sort themselves out on to the soils that suit them, so cause and effect cannot be inferred from simple observations.

What is required is an experimental approach. And also, because everyone agrees that if trees modify soil pH, it doesn't happen overnight, plenty of patience – which in practice means finding some trees that someone else planted sometime in the past. The best study that I know of was carried out in Poland by a joint Polish–American team and published in 2005 in the journal *Ecology Letters*. Replicate blocks of fourteen tree species (eight broadleaves and six conifers) had been planted in 1970, and the researchers went back 30 years later to see what had happened to the soil. Before the land was cleared for the experiment it was a Scots pine forest with an acid, sandy loam soil.

The effects of the different trees on the soil were dramatic. Underneath the conifers, the soil remained acid, and in some cases had become even more acid. The most acid soils were beneath Scots pine, Douglas fir, larch and

Austrian pine (*Pinus nigra*). Underneath the broadleaves, the soil generally became more alkaline, sometimes markedly so. The key variable turned out to be the amount of calcium in the leaves of the tree – the more calcium, the higher the soil pH. The tree with the most calcium-rich foliage, and which also produced the biggest rise in soil pH, was small-leaved lime, *Tilia cordata*, but sycamore and Norway maple weren't far behind.

The only important variable was foliage calcium, and once you know that, tree type itself (broadleaf or conifer, evergreen or deciduous) wasn't important. Thus although conifers generally lowered soil pH, and broadleaves raised it, the two groups overlapped. The conifer with the most calcium-rich leaves (silver fir, *Abies alba*) had about the same calcium as both pedunculate and red oak, and had a similar effect on soil pH. Hornbeam had even less calcium in its leaves, and produced the lowest soil pH of all the broadleaves. So the answer to the question 'do conifers make the soil below them more acid?' is generally yes, but there's a lot of variation between species, and not all conifers (or broadleaves) behave the same.

Moreover, there was evidence of positive feedback between trees and soil. They measured leaf calcium in 1995 and again in 2001, and found that trees with low-calcium leaves stayed the same, but the calcium content of calcium-rich leaves actually increased. So calcium in leaves raises soil pH, which further increases calcium in leaves, which raises soil pH … and so on. Finally, all this had a predictable effect on earthworms: in the soil beneath the high-calcium broadleaves, there were lots, of several species. Beneath pine and larch, there were essentially none.

There are lessons here for gardeners, even if they're not quite obvious. Don't imagine you can render a chalky soil rhododendron-friendly by planting a few pine trees – it simply takes too long. Remember too that an acid soil is a fragile thing, convertible overnight into an alkaline one by the addition of a few buckets of lime, so even the soil under an old pine tree may or may not be acid, depending on what else you, or a previous gardener, have been adding to the soil.

There's a lesson for composters too. For reasons that remain mysterious (to me anyway), the compost made from general garden waste often turns out to be surprisingly alkaline. But even if it takes ages to compost conifer needles, I think we can safely predict that the finished product will be acid.

. . . . . . ✳ . . . .

Crocks in pots

'[F]ill the bottom of the pot with extra drainage material, such as polystyrene pieces or crocks ...', says the RHS book *How to Garden*. Most people seem to agree: the BBC *Gardeners' World* website has instructions on planting up scores of different kinds of pots, but all begin with some variation on 'Place a layer of crocks in the bottom of the pot to improve drainage'.

So there you are, summer is just around the corner and you're happily chucking broken crocks into the bottom of a plant container before adding some compost. While you're doing this, 'textural discontinuities', 'capillary barriers' and 'funnelled flow' are probably not uppermost in your mind. But maybe they should be. Soil scientists, hydrologists and environmental engineers have long known that peculiar things happen at the junction between two layers of soil with different textures, and especially when a fine layer sits on top of a coarse layer. For example, scientists trying to track the movement of fertilisers, pesticides or other contaminants down soil profiles sometimes find that if the stuff they're following encounters such a discontinuity (especially if it's not perfectly level), it can stop heading downwards and zip off sideways, ending up a long way from where they expected to find it.

Fair enough, you may think, but what has that got to

with me, and can I go back to planting up my pots? Yes, in a minute, but first here's another funny thing. Because it resists compaction and provides good drainage, sand is the basis of most modern golf course putting greens. But the downside of sand is that it holds little water, dries out rapidly and needs a lot of watering. The most popular solution to this problem is around 300 mm of sand over a 100 mm layer of gravel. Capillary forces within the sand mean that water is unwilling to cross from the (relatively fine) sand to the (much coarser) gravel, creating what hydrologists and geologists call a 'perched' water table, essentially one that is higher up than it should be, and above the 'real' water table.

Maybe you're now starting to see the parallel between the sand and gravel beneath a putting green and the compost and crocks in your plant pot. Both are a fine layer over a coarse layer. But the former is designed to reduce water loss from the fine layer and keep it *wetter* than it would otherwise be, while the latter, if we believe the gardening books, is to improve drainage and keep the fine layer *drier*. They can't both be right, although in a sense they are. During heavy rain, the putting-green sand layer eventually becomes saturated, gravity overcomes capillary forces and the water has nowhere else to go but into the gravel, where it drains away rapidly. So the sand/gravel sandwich *is* well-drained. But once the surplus water has drained away, the sand remains wetter than it would be if it were just sitting on more sand.

Exactly the same happens in your plant pot. When you pour enough water in the top of the pot to saturate the compost, gravity overcomes the capillary barrier at the compost/crocks boundary and it drains away through the crocks and out of the drainage hole. But it would do exactly the same if the crocks weren't there, and when you stop watering, you're left with a perched water table in either case, crocks or no crocks. The only difference is that if there's a layer of crocks, the water table is perched at the compost/crocks boundary, and if there isn't, it's at the bottom of the pot. So there's no harm in continuing to bung crocks in the bottom of containers if you feel you ought to, or because your mother did, and her mother before her, but be aware that their only practical effect is to reduce the volume of compost available for plant roots. If you're worried about poor drainage, far better simply to add coarse grit or vermiculite to the compost.

What brings tears to my eyes is the number of perfectly good pots that must have been smashed over the years in the mistaken pursuit of improved drainage.

. . . . ❋ . . . .

Drought – not all bad news

I'm not going to waste my time trying to convince you that a drought is exactly a good thing, and clearly a proper, 1976-style drought is very bad news indeed, for all kinds of reasons. But purely from a gardening perspective, a bit less rain than usual is not all bad news. So on the principle that one should always look on the bright side, let me give you three reasons to welcome another fine, sunny day.

First of all, put your hand up if you really enjoy mowing the lawn. I thought so – not too many of you. Few things cause more angst than a brown lawn, but a dry lawn grows less than a wet one, and a brown lawn doesn't grow at all. Brown grass is not a sign that your lawn is dead, it's just the grass's natural way of shutting down until it rains again. Your grass will recover when it rains, and there is never any need to water an established lawn. And if you don't believe me, this is the official advice from the Turfgrass Growers Association (www.turfgrass.co.uk), who grow 70 per cent of the UK's turf between them, so they should know. In fact, watering your lawn during a drought does more harm than good. It encourages weeds and diseases, makes your soil more easily damaged by trampling, and encourages surface rooting, which means watering now makes your lawn more likely to suffer from drought in the future.

If you don't want your lawn to go brown in the first place, here are a few other things you can do: (1) keep your mower blades sharp; (2) apply an occasional light top-dressing of soil or compost; (3) don't use fertiliser: if your lawn isn't growing, it doesn't need feeding; (4) remove thatch with a lawn rake; and most important of all, (5) increase mowing height: taller grass has deeper roots, and also helps to shade and cool the ground. In time of drought, don't cut lower than 35–40 mm. Newly laid lawns *do* need watering, but only for the first month – after that they should be able to look after themselves.

Weeds need water just like other plants, and annual weeds, which need water for their seeds to germinate, are particularly dependent on rainfall. So less rain means fewer seedlings of hairy bittercress, groundsel, chickweed and annual meadow grass. Many perennial weeds rely mainly on seeds to get around too: think dandelions, willowherbs, docks, pearlwort and plantains. Not only do all these plants need water to germinate, wet soil makes their seedlings *much* harder to kill. There are few more unrewarding pastimes than hoeing seedlings of annual meadow grass on a wet day, only to return days later to find that most of them are still happily growing and flowering away. In dry weather there will be many fewer weed seedlings to start with, and when you kill them, they will stay dead.

Last but far from least, less rain means fewer slugs, or at any rate lower slug activity. In spring, when seeds are germinating and new shoots are just emerging, plants are at their most vulnerable to slugs. In fact slugs will eat seedlings of plants that they wouldn't (or couldn't) look at twice as mature plants. Even tree seedlings are in danger from slugs; in one Swedish study slugs wiped out over two-thirds of Scots pine seedlings, but only if it rained – in dry weather few seedlings were attacked.

The lesson is to water seedlings, young plants and anything newly planted, but to do so carefully, applying the water only where it's needed. Just spraying it everywhere will only attract slugs and persuade more weeds to germinate. Also try to water in the morning so that surface soil is dry by evening, which will discourage slugs. A useful discipline is to use a watering can – it's good practice for when your water company imposes a hosepipe ban, and the exercise will do you good.

· · · · · · ·❋· · · · · · · ·

Flooding – leave well alone

Whether it's flooded or not, it's a safe bet your garden is basically sodden,* and as far as your plants are concerned, the effect is much the same. A typical soil is about 50 per cent empty space, and most of the time, most of that space is filled with air. The space in soil may fill up briefly after rain, but the water quickly drains away, at least from the larger pores and channels. Which is just as well, since roots need air to breathe and, if the spaces in soil become filled with water for any length of time, they start to run out of oxygen. If that goes on for too long, the roots basically drown, and the plant dies.

As if that weren't bad enough, waterlogging also poisons plants. When microbes in the soil respire without oxygen, they produce a whole battery of nasty chemicals, including toxic quantities of heavy metals (such as manganese) and hydrogen sulphide. Which is why a waterlogged soil quickly starts to smell so horrible.

Plants that normally live in wet soils, or even in water, have evolved a variety of ways round a shortage of oxygen. Biochemical adaptations can make respiration more efficient and reduce the production of toxic by-products of anaerobic respiration, such as ethanol and acetaldehyde.

* This was written in the exceptionally wet winter of 2013/14.

But mostly what they do is make sure enough oxygen gets to the roots, via porous tissues or air-filled channels in their stems and roots. Some plants can also grow new *adventitious* roots at the surface of the soil, although obviously this doesn't help if you're actually underwater.

As far as the current soggy spell is concerned, there's bad news and good news. The bad news is that most plants are still dormant, which stops them making any active response to flooding. The good news is that because they're dormant, they're not doing much respiring anyway, so they can survive being flooded for a lot longer than they could in the summer. As long as the water, or at least most of it, drains away before active growth resumes in the spring, it's likely that not too much damage will be done. Even so, there may well be fatalities among plants from dry climates or of borderline hardiness, both of which are often particularly intolerant of sitting with their feet in water.

What can you do to help? In the longer term, the best thing you can do is try to improve your soil structure, and the easiest way of doing that is to add lots of organic matter, such as garden compost, chipped bark or shredded prunings. No need to dig it in, just add to the surface and let the worms do the rest. Not only will organic matter improve your soil drainage in its own right (and also, paradoxically, improve water retention in the summer if you have a sandy soil), but it will also give your earthworms plenty to eat, and many of the larger drainage pores and channels in soil are created by earthworms.

In the current crisis, there's not much you can do right now – indeed the less you do, the better. A good soil structure takes time to create but can be destroyed very quickly, especially by you walking on it, so keep off. In fact don't be tempted to do *anything* to your soil, such as planting new bare-root trees and shrubs, until the surplus water has drained away. If you dig a hole and it fills up with water, leave well alone.

. . . .❋. . . . .

Gardeners' Question Time, *part I*

I have to say that, owing to Eric Robson's almost unbearably arch chairmanship, I find *Gardeners' Question Time* quite a tough listen, so normally I don't bother. But if you ever do manage to sit through it, a fun thing to do is to spot those occasions when the panel just get it completely wrong. I first started to do this a year or two ago when a woman enquired if there was something wrong with her oak tree, which had failed to produce any acorns for the last three or four years. The panel gave a typical 'gardening' response to this question, based on the assumption that any self-respecting plant should flower and fruit every year. Maybe a late frost had damaged the flowers? Maybe the poor thing needed watering, or feeding? No consensus was reached, but the unfortunate woman was left in no doubt that something was up, and what's more, it was time she did something about it, even if no one was exactly sure what.

In fact oaks, and many other forest trees, indulge in *mast seeding*, named for the old word 'mast' for beech seeds. Beech is a notorious mast seeder, which means it produces good crops of seed only at intervals. In beech itself good seed crops may be very infrequent indeed, sometimes a decade or more apart. Oak isn't quite so shy, and may even produce a crop of acorns in two, or even three, successive years, but then give up for five years or more. Botanists still aren't 100 per cent sure why trees do this, but the key is that all the beech or oak trees in a region are synchronised, which strongly suggests it's evolved to outfox seed predators like mice. During the lean years the mouse population is reduced to a low level, which is then overwhelmed by the unexpected bounty of a mast year, so most seeds survive. If, instead, oaks produced a moderate crop of acorns every year, then mice and other seed predators would be able to eat most of them. But why they do it isn't really important; the point is that an oak tree that doesn't produce any acorns for a few years is just doing what oak trees do.

Another interesting example took place a few weeks ago, in Carrickfergus in County Antrim, when a questioner wondered what to do about his lawn, which had apparently been overrun by rushes. Again the panel were quick to suggest remedies, of a more or less drastic nature, and all based on the common knowledge that rushes = wet, therefore drainage must need improving. But hang on a minute. *Rushes*? When did you last – indeed when did you ever – see a lawn with rushes in it? We looked at the composition of over 50 private lawns in Sheffield a few years ago and found not a single rush, for one very good reason. *Juncus effusus* or soft rush, by far our commonest species, is a tall plant that is quite intolerant of regular mowing. It would be an interesting lawn that had soft rush in it, and if rushes really were the problem, the best advice would be to buy a new lawnmower, or at least use the existing one a bit more often.

So what was our questioner on about? Since no one bothered to enquire further, we will never know, but my guess is that his lawn was full of field *woodrush*, *Luzula campestris*. Unlike their close relatives, woodrushes are short plants that are quite at home in lawns, especially ones on acid soils, and there are plenty of lawns here in Sheffield (a city of acid soils) that have nearly as much woodrush as grass. Woodrushes are not plants of wet soils, so drainage is not the problem, and in fact I'm not sure there *is* a problem. Woodrushes are short, rather grass-like plants, and if you don't look at them too closely, you might well think they were grasses. So my advice to those with woodrush-infested lawns is the same as my advice to those whose oak trees haven't produced any acorns for a few years: if that's the worst that ever happens to your garden, then you're luckier than most of us.

· · · · · · · ❋ · · · · · · ·

Gardeners' Question Time, *part II*

GQT are at it again. The flowers on a listener's newly planted New Dawn rose had opened white instead of pink. Was this, she wanted to know, perhaps something to do with this year's wet summer? Specifically, had all that rain washed the potassium out of the soil, and was it this lack of potassium that had led to this peculiar colour change? This hypothesis drew a murmur of approval from the *GQT* panel, as though flowers losing their colour through lack of potassium was a well-known, everyday occurrence.

But how likely is it that less (or more) nutrients or water in the soil can change the colour of a plant's flowers? One way to answer that question is to appeal to our collective experience. We've all, over the years, grown a lot of plants. We've also all seen those plants experience everything from heavy rain to drought, and also receive lots of fertiliser, or none at all, in soils of very variable fertility. Has any of this ever caused a plant to produce flowers that were a different colour from those we were expecting? I doubt it, although if it has happened, I'm sure someone will soon let me know.

A different approach is to query the scientific literature. Is there any published record of anyone changing the colour of the flowers of New Dawn (or of any rose, or of any plant, come to that) by manipulating potassium concentration? There is not, and bear in mind that if you could, plant breeders and growers would have written about it by now. Not only that, you can be sure they would be routinely using it to manipulate flower colour. Flower colour *can* be modified by the environment, as the RHS book *Science and the Garden* reports. Broadly, low light leads to less intense colours, and low temperatures to more intense colours. But potassium? No.

Not that flower colours are immutable. Red/blue changes are quite common, in morning glories and pulmonarias for example, but this happens by the plant adjusting the internal cellular pH of its flowers, and there isn't much you can do to stop it, or to make it happen any faster. The only flower colour you can readily influence is in hydrangeas, which are blue in acid soil and red in alkaline. If you have trouble remembering this, recall the behaviour of litmus paper back in school chemistry, and then try to remember that hydrangeas are the opposite way round.

So what did cause the listener's white flowers? I can think of at least three alternative explanations, listed here in order of increasing probability:

1. Most roses are grafted, and if for some reason the scion has died, shoots from the rootstock might have flowers of a different colour. But the commonest rootstock does not have white flowers, and anyway the flowers of the rootstock are likely to look quite different in size and shape, not just colour.

2. It may just have been the wrong plant. Between them, nurseries and garden centres label plants wrongly surprisingly often. This is particularly likely in the case of roses bought while not in flower, when they all do tend to look pretty similar.

3. New Dawn flowers are pale pink only when newly opened, and fade as they age to almost white, or at best cream. It's possible, if one were seduced by a picture in a catalogue or on a website into expecting a stronger pink, that New Dawn could easily look almost white. Especially in this year's dull summer, when they are likely to have been even paler than usual.

There are lessons here for *GQT* panellists. Just because a listener has a theory about their problem, that doesn't mean it's right. And if you don't know the answer to a question, just say so.

. . . . ❋ . . . .

Meadows and nutrients

Ever wondered why that wildflower meadow you tried to make turned out such a mess? The answer almost certainly has something to do with soil nutrients. Not just any old nutrient either, but one in particular: phosphorus. Fifteen years ago, a consortium of European ecologists looked at the relationship between soil nutrients and floristic diversity in 281 European meadows, and found a striking result: diversity was totally controlled by soil phosphorus (P). Below 5 mg of P per 100 g of soil, there were up to 60 different species of plants in 100 square metres of meadow. Above that figure (up to 35 mg), no meadow contained more than twenty species. Not only that, the twenty species that were present were pretty dull; rare and interesting wildflowers were confined to low-P soils.

Why phosphorus? Why not, for example, nitrogen, an element that plants need in really large quantities? Well, nitrogen is a bit of a fly-by-night, here-today-gone-tomorrow kind of element. Nitrate is very soluble in water, so it's easily washed out of soils by rain, and an army of microbes are just itching to turn it back into gaseous nitrogen, but it can be quickly replenished by the breakdown of soil organic matter. In fact soil nitrogen varies so much on a daily, almost hourly, basis that it's quite hard to pin down exactly how much there is in soil. On the other hand, once phosphorus gets into soil, it's there to stay; P ions are tightly bound to clays and other soil minerals, and released only very slowly. We can still identify soils that were last cultivated by the Romans because they have more phosphorus than soils that have never been cultivated.

How do garden soils compare to the soils beneath meadows? Well, almost any survey of European garden soils tells the same story, but a recent study in Flanders (northern Belgium), published in the journal *Landscape and Urban Planning*, is typical. Out of 1,817 soil samples from Flemish gardens, only 2.6 per cent had less than 5 mg P. Almost half had more than 30 mg, and over a fifth had more than 50 mg, which is practically off the scale even for a fertile agricultural soil. As the researchers themselves put it, 'These (very) high concentrations of phosphorus are probably due to excessive fertilization', and 'they do indicate that gardeners on average could do with less phosphorus fertilization'. You can, as they say, say that again.

What is true for wild meadows is true for your garden – phosphorus levels of 30, 40 or even 50 mg encourage the growth of big, fast-growing plants like coarse grasses, nettles and docks to such an extent that more interesting, slower-growing wildflowers just don't stand a chance.

If you'd like to establish a wildflower meadow and your soil has too much phosphorus – and most do – then what can you do? The short-term – but very drastic – solution is to pay someone to take your topsoil away, or at least most of it, and start again with the subsoil, which is usually low in nutrients. For those with more patience, cutting and removing the vegetation every year will – slowly – run down the phosphorus in the soil. Growing greedy crops like potatoes and brassicas – *without* adding any fertiliser – may speed things up, but even then it will be a slow business. Eventually, sowing parasitic yellow-rattle, which targets coarse grasses, may help, but experience suggests you need to get very high levels of soil fertility down first.

In the meantime, don't forget that your garden got the way it is because someone (if not you, then your predecessor) used too much fertiliser. Your garden needs less fertiliser than you think it does. Finally, a recent study in Minnesota, where use of phosphorus fertiliser is restricted by law, found that 84 per cent of phosphorus inputs to gardens came from pet waste. I'm not advising you what to do about that, I just thought you ought to know.

. . . .❋. . . . .

Meadows and sugar

Given the current fuss about dietary sugar, you may well have a cupboard full of the stuff that you're too frightened to eat. If so, one solution might be to tip it on the garden.

And if you think that's a silly idea, read on. I've mentioned before that, in the average garden, the biggest barrier to establishing an interesting wildflower meadow is high soil fertility. The quick but extremely drastic solution is to remove the topsoil and start again with the subsoil. Easier, but much slower, is to cut and remove the vegetation every year. Sowing yellow-rattle, which parasitises coarse grasses, will help in the end, but not unless you can reduce high levels of soil fertility first.

But if your soil is too fertile, there is one other, and slightly surprising, technical fix. The plants in your garden compete for soil nutrients not only with each other, but also with an army of soil microbes. Normally this competition is a bit one-sided because the plants have a ready supply of carbon (from photosynthesis) that allows them to grow lots of roots. Microbes, in contrast, have no independent supply of carbon and have to make do with decomposing organic matter, plus whatever they can borrow or steal from the plants. This is never as much as they would like, so they are permanently undernourished.

You can level the playing field by supplying some extra carbon, and the simplest way to do this is to add some sugar. This gives soil microbes a shot in the arm, so they grow faster and compete more effectively with the plants for nutrients. The total amount of soil nutrients doesn't change, but there's less for the plants, so they grow more slowly and biomass goes down.

Although we've known about this for a long time, I was always worried that the effect might be rather short-lived, but a new study from Estonia, published in the *Journal of Vegetation Science*, shows that it isn't. The researchers added sugar every year to a hay meadow and showed that after ten years, the weight of vegetation was much lower and the amount of bare ground greater in plots treated with sugar than in control plots.

They also added fertiliser to other plots, which had a predictable effect: biomass went up and diversity went down. The big winner in fertilised plots was our old friend couch grass. The effect of sugar on diversity, on the other hand, was disappointing. Despite the lower biomass, diversity didn't change much, and after ten years there were only subtle differences between control plots and those treated with sugar.

To try to find out why, they added seeds of the common plantain, *Plantago lanceolata*. Again predictably, none of the plantain seedlings in the fertilised plots survived. This is one of the main reasons diversity is so low in grasslands on fertile soils: competition from established plants completely prevents any new plants establishing from seed. Some seedlings survived in both control and sugar-treated plots, but more survived in the latter.

What the plantain results show is that the failure of diversity to increase naturally in these plots is most likely a dispersal problem; there simply aren't many other species around. In a garden, of course, you would probably want to add something more interesting and attractive than plantains. But they illustrate the key principle: if you want to brighten up some dull grassland by sowing seeds of wildflowers, adding sugar gives them a fighting chance; without it, they will probably fail. You should also, of course, cut and remove the hay every year, traditionally in late summer.

In case you're wondering, the researchers added 1 kg of sugar per square metre every year, at the end of May and the beginning of September (500 g each time). Also, not only does the effect persist as long as sugar is added, it also happens very quickly; if you add sugar in spring, plant growth will already be reduced by the summer.

· · · · · · ··✳·· · · · · · ·

Mulch

'A mixture of wet straw, leaves, etc., spread around (the roots of) a plant to enrich or insulate the soil' is the definition of mulch in my *Shorter Oxford Dictionary*, which throws into sharp relief the limitations of dictionaries. Neither wet straw nor leaves are necessarily ideal mulch materials, and there's a lot more to mulching than enrichment and insulation.

So what should we be mulching with, and what can we expect it to do for us? For the average gardener, the primary function of mulch – which does not appear in the above definition – is weed control. Indeed, for the gardener determined to eschew herbicides and who doesn't want to spend all summer hoeing, mulch is *the* weed-control technique of choice. Almost anything that covers the soil will control weeds to some extent, and in the world of commercial horticulture, mulch can be almost anything, from plastic to 'living mulch' such as clover. But plastic is unsightly, and living mulches can cause as many problems as they solve; in a garden context, mulch is usually a layer of some kind of organic material. Since most weed seeds need light to germinate, any layer thick enough to exclude light (which isn't much) will prevent most weeds from germinating. If it's thick enough, it will also kill any weed seedlings that do germinate.

So how thick is enough, or to put it another way, how long is a piece of string? Plenty of weeds have quite small seeds, and for these even 2 cm (¾ inch) is fatal. But weeds with big seeds, goosegrass, say, will come through that as though it wasn't there, so 10 cm (4 in) is a useful minimum to aim for. Wild oat seedlings will come through 20 cm, so it's just as well wild oat isn't a garden weed, but you get the idea: for weed control, the thicker the better. Of course there's nothing to stop seeds of dandelions and willowherbs blowing in and growing on top of the mulch, but at least weeds rooted in mulch are easy to uproot.

On the other hand, don't even think about trying to control established perennial weeds with mulch. Creeping thistle shoots can emerge from roots at a depth of a metre or more, so a few extra centimetres on top is basically water off a duck's back.

The downside of mulch, of course, is that it will also 'control' plants you want to grow. Shrubs aren't a problem, and robust perennials will shrug off 4 inches of mulch, but don't cover small plants with thick layers. You're often advised to apply mulch in spring, but this conflicts with a stronger imperative not to dump mulch on top of grow-ing plants, so autumn is better – *after* herbaceous plants have finished growing, and *after* some rain, but *before* soil is chilled by winter, so the soil under the mulch is moist and still relatively warm.

What to use? Cost, aesthetics and function all come into play. Despite what they say, there is such a thing as a free mulch, so start with whatever free materials are to hand: garden compost, shredded prunings, lawn mowings, fallen leaves, shredded paper, or a mixture of all of them. If you have a large supply of raw material, lots of hedges for example, a shredder is a worthwhile investment for the would-be mulcher. Some mulches look a lot nicer than others, so put whatever you prefer to look at on the top, which will often be compost. The appearance of leaves is greatly improved if they are left to rot for a year or two before use. Weed control will be improved by starting with a base layer of a few sheets of unshredded newspaper.

Few gardens produce enough home-grown mulch, so you may decide to buy some. Despite the dictionary definition, straw is not a good idea. Wet straw may be well behaved, but dry straw isn't, and unless it's certified organic, you never know what may be in it. Bark mulch is heavily promoted and looks nice, but tree bark is naturally waterproof, so bark mulch does not absorb and retain water. Chipped softwood absorbs water and is generally cheaper than bark, so should be your first choice. Wood is heavy stuff, so distance is the key to cost; shop around locally for the cheapest supplier. If you have a friendly local sawmill and you're prepared to collect it yourself, it may cost very little at all. You may also find sawdust available very cheaply, but sawdust should be avoided – its fine texture means it tends to form a compact, water-repellent layer, and it looks awful too. Fresh wood chips can look a bit garish and 'municipal' too, but they soon darken and become less conspicuous with age.

Weed control may be your primary aim, but all organic mulches do a lot more than that for your garden. They slowly decay, adding organic matter to your soil, encouraging earthworms and improving soil structure and water-holding capacity, thus aiding deep and extensive rooting. They also physically protect the soil surface from heavy rain, while allowing rainwater to percolate slowly through into the soil, preventing run-off and erosion. And, while you shouldn't tread on your soil if you can help it, chunky, coarse mulches will also protect it from feet. Even carbon-rich mulches like wood chips contain small amounts of nutrients that gradually build up the fertility of your soil. You will often read that such mulches 'rob' your soil of nitrogen as they decay, but this is really only likely if you physically incorporate large amounts into the soil; apply mulch to the surface, let the worms do the rest, and there won't be a problem.

Two final pieces of advice. Don't apply mulch right up to the stems of trees and shrubs, and for permanent weed control, keep an eye on your mulch and top up as necessary to maintain a thick layer.

. . . .❀.. . . . .

Soil type

When it comes to what you can grow in your garden (and more importantly, what you can't), few things are as important as soil. Especially because, to a very large extent, you are stuck with the soil Mother Nature has given you.

The two big variables are texture and pH. Let's look at pH first, because it's simpler and easier to change – although only in one direction. You can test your pH with a simple DIY kit, which is good enough for most purposes. Meters with a metal probe you stick in the soil are too unreliable to be recommended. Alternatively, you could just check what your neighbours are growing. If they're all happily growing ericaceous plants like rhododendrons, and other lime-haters like camellias, you have an acid soil. If *no one* is growing those kinds of plants, you probably have a soil around neutral (pH 7), or even an alkaline soil (pH above 7). For most plants, including the majority of fruit and vegetables, a neutral to mildly acid soil (pH 6–7) is ideal. If you have an acid soil, raising the pH is quick and easy – just add lime. If you have an alkaline soil, lowering the pH is difficult and slow. Adding sulphur or persistent use of ammonium sulphate fertiliser may work in the end, but will take years or even decades. If there's free limestone or chalk in your soil (if it fizzes when you pour vinegar on it), then there's no realistic hope of lowering the pH.

Texture is more subtle, but just as important. Essentially this is the size of the mineral particles in your soil, from coarse (sandy soil) to very fine (clay soil). The soil we would all like – a loam – has a nice mix of soil particle sizes. A sandy soil is well drained, which is both good and bad. Large-leaved moisture lovers like ligularias and hostas will struggle, but a sandy soil is easy to work, and borderline hardy plants will love not having soggy roots in the winter. Generally, drought-tolerant plants will do best in a sandy soil, but a wide range of plants can be grown once you get them established. A clay soil holds lots of water and nutrients, so tends to be fertile but awkward to work with – it sets like rock when dry, and is easily smeared or compacted when wet. Mulching with plenty of organic matter will improve both sandy *and* clay soils.

How do you tell what sort of soil you have? The simple solution is to get hold of a handful and squeeze it. If it just falls to pieces, you have a sandy soil, if you can mould it like plasticine, you have a clay soil, while loam is intermediate.

But if you don't want to get your hands dirty, or you're thinking of moving and want to know what your new soil might be like, there's an alternative. The National Soil Resources Institute at Cranfield University provide an online soil map (www.landis.org.uk/soilscapes), which really does tell you everything you need to know. For example, both RHS Wisley and my garden have acid (but not very acid) soil, although I have to say that there the resemblance ends. But the Cranfield map fills in all the important detail. It tells me that the soils where I live are 'slow permeable, seasonally wet, acid loams and clays', and further explains that their drainage is rather poor and their natural fertility rather low. Wisley's soil, on the other hand, is 'freely draining, slightly acid sandy'. Both descriptions are absolutely spot on, and go a long way towards explaining why Wisley doesn't have much trouble with slugs, and why I do.

Give it a try, but I warn you that if you have even the slightest interest in soil, you'll find it (like much on the internet) seriously addictive.

· · · · · · · ·❋· · · · · · · ·

Sunburned leaves?

Two years ago, four Hungarian scientists published a paper called 'Optics of sunlit water drops on leaves: conditions under which sunburn is possible' in the journal *New Phytologist*. Given the near-universal belief that water drops can scorch plant leaves on a sunny day (e.g. the RHS book *How to Garden*: 'Under a hot midday sun, water droplets on leaves will act as miniature magnifying glasses and may scorch them'), you may be surprised – or you may not

– that no one had previously checked to see if this actually happens.

First of all, the short answer is that it doesn't. At various times on a hot, cloudless day in July (in Hungary, where such things still happen), water drops were carefully placed on the surface of horizontal ginkgo and Norway maple leaves and left in the sun until they had evaporated, which generally took an hour or two. Careful examination of the leaves revealed no trace of any damage.

Which leaves the interesting question: since water drops undoubtedly can act as small lenses capable of focusing the sun's rays, why do they fail to cause any damage? To find out, the researchers carefully calculated the paths of light rays falling on water drops. The first thing to say is that water makes a less effective lens than glass, owing to its lower refractive index. The second is that the shapes of water drops on a leaf vary a lot, depending on how 'wettable' the leaf surface is. On a wettable leaf, such as maple, water spreads out to form a thin, shallow drop. Although such a drop is capable of acting as a lens, it focuses light well below the leaf surface (or it would if the leaf were transparent – in practice it doesn't focus it anywhere). On a less wettable leaf, such as ginkgo or rowan, water forms drops that are more nearly spherical, but these still focus light that comes from directly above well below the leaf. Such drops *can* focus light from a low angle on to the leaf beside the drop, but only (assuming the leaf is horizontal) early or late in the day, when the light intensity is low. In any case, such drops easily roll off leaves, which are rarely still or exactly horizontal, so the likelihood of causing sunburn is very low. As the authors conclude, 'water drops cannot cause sunburn, either on water-repellent or on wettable leaves'.

Are there any circumstances under which water drops on leaves can cause sunburn? Yes, but only if the leaf has a dense covering of water-repellent hairs, in which case drops can be held *above* the leaf surface, allowing them to focus light on the surface itself. The researchers were able to demonstrate such damage on the leaves of the floating fern *Salvinia natans*, which has such hairs, if they were kept still in a small container of water. But terrestrial plants with similar hairs shed water drops very quickly, again making sunburn extremely unlikely in practice. In any case, most plants with densely hairy leaves are drought-tolerant, so why do you feel the need to water them anyway?

None of this should occasion much surprise. Since thundery summer rain is often followed by bright sunshine, if this really caused sunburn, the leaves of most plants would be full of burn holes most of the time, and they're not, are they?

Given the unambiguously negative evidence, why is the belief that water drops can cause sunburn so persistent, and advice to that effect dispensed even by authoritative sources like the RHS? One possibility is that although the researchers used plain tap water, many less pleasant liquids can find their way on to leaves: drops of acid rain, sea water, chlorinated water, 'grey' water, fertiliser or other chemicals. All of these can leave deposits on leaves that *look* like scorch marks, or may actually dehydrate leaf patches by osmosis, causing burn-like spots.

Even though you don't need to worry about sunburn, it probably is a good idea to avoid watering during the middle of the day – especially in sunny or windy weather – since this may lead to excessive water loss by evaporation. The optimal watering time is early morning, since evening watering can mean leaves and growing points remaining sodden all night, which can encourage fungal pathogens.

The original scientific paper led to a lot of press attention at the time. Here's how the news was greeted by the *Daily Mail*: 'Sun shining? Then don't water your plants or you'll burn them.' The lesson is clear: don't believe everything you read in the papers.

· · · · · · · ·❋· · · · · · · ·

Wildflowers and poor soil

Read almost any gardening book or website, and sooner or later you will encounter the following phrase, or something very like it: 'wildflowers thrive in poor soil'. But is that true? Is it even likely?

The problem is that there is no real distinction between wild flowers and garden flowers. It's true that many garden plants are complex hybrids or selections with sterile, double flowers and exist only in gardens. But it's equally true that many are more or less identical to the original wild species, even if that species is wild in Japan or America rather than in the UK. The acid test is that if I see a plant I've never seen before and try to guess if it's a 'garden plant' or a 'wildflower', much of the time I wouldn't have a clue. In other words, there is no operational definition of 'wildness' or 'gardenness', nothing about a plant you can measure to determine its degree of wildness. And, as a general principle, all such unmeasurable categories should be treated with deep suspicion. 'Native' and 'alien' is another good example, and worst of all, 'fashionable' and 'unfashionable'.

In reality, a plant's liking for a fertile soil depends on the sort of soil it evolved to grow in. Plants that evolved in rich soils like rich soils, in the sense that if you give them lots of fertiliser they will reward you by growing faster and bigger. Plants that evolved in poor soils (which in fact is most of the world's plants) have adapted to manage without lots of nutrients. Part of that adaptation is to grow slowly, and such plants cannot be persuaded to grow fast, however much fertiliser you give them. The imaginary distinction between wildflowers and garden plants cuts across this divide at right angles, and gardeners grow lots of both kinds. For example, the rock garden and alpine house are populated almost entirely by small, slow-growing plants that will remain small and slow-growing however kind you are to them. On the other hand, the vegetable plot is mostly full of fast-growing plants that respond well to fertiliser, not least because slow-growing plants never attracted the attention of those on the lookout for a meal. It's also worth mentioning that, whether we like it or not, we all grow one group of plants that really love fertile soils; if you use lots of fertiliser you will certainly have lots of big, happy weeds.

Wildflowers and garden plants *do* differ, but the difference lies not in the plants themselves, but in the way we try to grow them. We generally grow garden plants in quite rich soils, which would soon allow the bigger and more territorially ambitious sorts to crush their neighbours. Recognising this, we vigorously police our borders, weeding, thinning and dividing in an attempt (not always successful) to prevent the thugs from taking over. But we generally grow wildflowers in some sort of 'meadow', where we give them free rein to compete not only with each other, but also with other plants, especially grasses. Under these conditions, the struggle that we take such care to prevent in the border goes to its logical and (on a fertile soil) unattractive conclusion.

So, do 'wildflowers thrive in poor soil'? No, not really, any more than you or I would thrive on a diet of bread and water. A better way to look at it is that wildflowers don't like poor soils very much, but the grasses that would like to overwhelm them like them even less.

. . . . ❋ . . . .

Hot beds

If you grow vegetables, you already know some of the crucial requirements: a fertile soil and adequate water for starters. You also know that, in a temperate climate like Britain, warmth is vital; nothing will grow outdoors in winter. You probably worry less about light, and usually of course you don't need to, because light tends to vary in tandem with temperature. Normally if there's enough light, it's warm enough too.

Normally, but not always. By the end of April, day-length is the same as in early August, but in the vegetable garden the two seasons couldn't look more different. August (usually anyway) looks and feels like summer, with crops of all sorts growing away like mad. The end of April can feel like summer too, at least on a good day, but the vegetable plot at this time is a study in brown, with lots of bare ground, and most new-season crops little more than seedlings. The problem is that until sometime in April, depending on exactly where you live, the soil and air are both too cold for seeds to germinate and for plants to grow. There may be fifteen hours of daylight every day by the end of April, but most of it is wasted.

There are, of course, ways to try to get ahead of the game. You can grow crops in a greenhouse, or on a windowsill, and then plant them out later, but the scale of both is limited. Yet there is a potential source of free heat in the garden: any heap of decaying organic matter, as long as it's big enough, will get hot and stay that way for weeks or even months. You may well have wondered vaguely if all that heat could be used to grow early crops, but have been unsure how to make that work in practice.

Don't worry – someone else has endured the years of trial and error needed to devise a practical 'hot bed' system, so that you don't have to. His name is Jack First, and the fruits of his experience are distilled in a little book called simply *Hot Beds*. Essentially the technique requires a bed of decomposing material, with a frame on top to contain the growing medium, and a transparent glass or polythene 'light' on top to keep the heat in. You could buy all the kit, but the book provides detailed instructions for making your own. Using the methods described, the author routinely harvests radishes, rocket and salad leaves in early March, lettuce and turnips in late March, and carrots, beetroot and even potatoes in April and May. And all that in Keighley too – not the warmest or sunniest place in the world.

Books like this sometimes strike me as not particularly realistic, unless you're prepared to live what amounts to one long episode of *The Good Life*. But Jack shows every sign of realising that although many of us may strive for perfection, few of us will achieve it. So, for example, although the core of the traditional method is stable manure, he has plenty of suggestions for those of us who can't get hold of the genuine article. The method will work with leaves, paper, cardboard, wood shavings, sawdust, straw and even old cotton and wool clothes – anything, in fact, that could go on the compost heap. Some of these materials are low in nitrogen, but we all produce over a litre of the remedy for that every day.

Similarly, the details of frame ventilation sound at first so complicated that it's hard to see how they could be achieved by anyone with a normal life, but it turns out that such attention to detail isn't strictly necessary. Jack First set up six hot beds at schools around Keighley, and all managed to produce decent early crops, despite a lack of expert attention, staff illness, school holidays and even vandalism. Hot beds are obviously quite forgiving.

Just one final point. It's obviously a bad idea for crops to squash up against the lights as they grow taller, and to avoid this First recommends gradually jacking up the frames with bits of wood. But an alternative solution is to replace the lights with plastic cloches; visit the National Trust's Acorn Bank Garden near Penrith to see this system in operation.

········ ❋ ········

Real meadows

A day or two after the end of last year's summer opening season, I visited Stillingfleet Lodge Gardens, a few miles south of York. It is a delightful small garden, basically cottage garden in style, with many unusual plants and chickens, and just one startling bit of rectangular modernity to keep you on your toes. 'Worth a long journey to visit' says the RHS, and I wouldn't disagree at all.

One of Stillingfleet's many joys is a real wildflower meadow. 'Real' in two senses. First, it actually is a meadow, in the sense of an area of perennial grass and wildflowers, managed by annual cutting. Second, it is a genuine agricultural survival, with a history as permanent grassland that probably goes back centuries, and which has simply been incorporated into a modern garden. In the jargon of the

National Vegetation Classification, it's a proper piece of MG5, the species-rich, unimproved grassland that used to be found all over Britain, but is now very rare.

So it clearly saddens Vanessa Cook, Stillingfleet's owner and creator, to discover that some visitors find her meadow a bit dull. A clue to why can be found in a recent issue of *The Garden*, where Nigel Colborn reports that a visitor to his garden asked why his meadow had no wild poppies in it. Nigel had to explain, kindly and tactfully I'm sure, that no meadow since the dawn of time has had poppies in it, and that poppies belong in cornfields.

Both Nigel and Vanessa's slightly dissatisfied visitors have been seduced by the rise of the 'annual meadow', the drifts of annuals that have become increasingly popular recently. The problem is that for sheer flowering firepower, annuals are simply unbeatable, because flowering is what annuals are all about. For an annual, the only route to immortality is to produce lots and lots of flowers, and thus large numbers of seeds, and to waste as little time and effort as possible on anything else. But perennials, whether woody or herbaceous, have other things on their minds. A perennial may, briefly, be smothered in flowers, but it can't keep that up for long. Essentially it has to spend scarce resources on the things that will ensure its survival next year, and the year after that – which is, basically, roots. If you're ever unsure about whether a plant is an annual or a perennial, a quick test is to get hold of it and pull. An annual will come out of the ground with relatively little effort, while a perennial – unless very young – will not.

Real MG5 contains only native plants, which in the countryside is as it should be. In a garden, you can pep up a meadow with all kinds of non-native perennials, but you can never really compete with the show put on by a community of annuals. Indeed, if you ever encounter a perennial that looks like it's broken the rules, it's always a good idea to approach its claims of perenniality with some scepticism. The latest in a long line of examples is *Digitalis* 'Illumination Pink', Chelsea Plant of the Year in 2012, which claims to be perennial *and* smothered in flowers for months. All the plants *Which? Gardening* grew did flower for months, but none of them survived the following winter.

The problem is that 'annual meadows', whatever they are, are not meadows; they don't look like meadows, and nor are they managed like meadows. Nigel Colborn is so dissatisfied with 'annual meadow' that he has decided to call his drift of poppies, cornflowers, corn marigolds and corn cockles 'the arable'. Sadly, I can't see that catching on, but can anyone think of anything better?

· · · · · · · ✳ · · · · · · · ·

Sweet peas

If you want to grow sweet peas, and you're wondering which varieties to grow, who do you ask? This question occurred to me when, by chance, *The Garden* and *Which? Gardening* recently came up with their sweet pea recommendations at almost the same time. Since the RHS have a committee for every day of the year, they naturally enough went to their Sweet Pea Advisory Group and asked them to come up with a list. They turn out to be fans of Spencers (large, frilly flowers on long stems, excellent for cut flowers), so therefore we have a relatively long list (24) of recommended Spencer sweet peas. As a result grandifloras (non-frilly flowers on shorter stems) don't get much of a mention, but the Advisory Group do have a soft spot for semi-grandifloras, which combine a good, old-fashioned scent with long stems: 'Albutt Blue' is singled out for praise.

Which? adopted their typically somewhat more democratic approach. They started by asking sweet pea experts for their recommendations, although we don't know who these experts were, or how many. This produced a longlist, which was then whittled down to 30 varieties. These were sown at Capel Manor Gardens in north London and the plants monitored for vigour, number of flowers, pests and diseases and how well they lasted as cut flowers. Visitors to the gardens were also asked to choose their favourite, and the final result was thirteen recommended varieties.

How do the lists compare? *Which?* weren't so sold on Spencers, so their list included two heritage varieties, 'King Size Navy Blue' and 'Matucana', plus one 'modern grandiflora', 'High Scent'. All three had a strong scent, but weren't much good as cut flowers. *Which?* also liked 'Albutt Blue'. The remaining nine Spencers recommended by *Which?* had just three in common with *The Garden*'s longer list of 24: 'Sir Jimmy Shand', 'Jilly' and 'Valerie Harrod'. The first two sound pretty good to me, and were excellent as cut flowers, but 'Valerie Harrod' hasn't much scent, which means it's a waste of space as far as I'm concerned. Honestly, is anything more disappointing than a sweet pea with little or no scent? That's a rhetorical question, but I'll answer it anyway: yes, a rose with no scent.

Mostly, *Which?* didn't try *The Garden*'s recommendations and find them wanting, they simply didn't try them. Only one of *The Garden*'s 24 was grown by *Which?* but rejected: 'White Frills' suffered badly from pests and diseases in their trial.

So where does that leave us? In the first place, putting the two lists together, 'Matucana', and 'High Scent' look like the varieties to go for if you really want the best scent. 'Albutt Blue', 'Sir Jimmy Shand' and 'Jilly' look good choices if you want cut flowers, but plenty of scent too. But bear in mind that 'Albutt Blue' is anything but blue, in fact it's pale lavender. But mostly what the two lists suggest to me is that there are simply too many sweet pea varieties around to expect a consensus, and more introduced every year.

The Garden and *Which?* agree on two things. First, that those of you who hanker after a highly scented red sweet pea are likely to be disappointed. *Which?* grew three red varieties and found they had almost no scent. *The Garden* recommends two red varieties, 'Winston Churchill' and 'Ruby Anniversary', but says the former has a 'light scent', and doesn't mention the scent of the latter at all. And second, that although you can sow sweet peas in spring or autumn, if you want the best flowers for the longest time, October is the month.

········ ✳ ········

The value of trees

You may value a tree, in your garden or in the street, for any number of reasons: for the wildlife it supports, or its shade on a hot day, or simply because it's beautiful. But can we put a number on that value? In short, what is a tree worth?

Plenty of people have asked themselves the same question, especially in climates with hot summers, where people tend to spend a lot of money on air conditioning, and therefore shade is a valuable commodity. In California, Sacramento's community-owned electricity utility – with the delightful acronym SMUD – have an online tree benefit estimator (https://usage.smud.org/treebenefit/) that will estimate the number of kWh (and thus the amount of CO_2) saved by any given tree. You could use this to put a value on an existing tree, or predict the value of a new tree you are thinking of planting. SMUD will then give you a free tree, and their website has lots of good advice on looking after your new tree.

SMUD's benefit estimator makes clear that tree location is crucial, in ways that aren't always obvious. For example, you might think that south of the house would be the best place for a tree, but it's not. Because shadows are short around midday, unless it's very big, or very near the house, a south-positioned tree doesn't shade the house very much. Trees on the west side of a house are by far the most valuable, because they provide long shadows in late afternoon when the air is hottest, which is also when people return home from work and switch on the air conditioning. From SMUD's perspective, coping with this peak demand is expensive.

But even trees in the 'wrong' place may shade another property. Recent research in Toronto, another city with hot summers and lots of air conditioning, found that about half the shade benefit of urban trees was received by houses not on the plot where the tree was actually growing. What's more, they found that worrying too much about the perfect strategic location of a tree was a mistake; urban trees typically have quite a high mortality rate, so in practice it's best to focus on choosing the best spot from a purely 'gardening' perspective, i.e. where the tree is most likely to thrive. As long as your neighbours are doing this too, everyone benefits. Nor should you think you are doing this only for the benefit of someone who will own the house after you have moved on; even young trees provide significant shade, especially if you choose a fast-growing tree like a birch.

Of course, shade may not seem a priority in a predominantly dull, cool country like Britain, although we may change our minds if climate change continues and we get more hot summers like 2003.* In any case, trees may provide many other benefits, such as improving air quality, reducing storm-water flooding, decreasing noise and increasing privacy, among others. It's not easy to include all these benefits in a single measurement, but one way is to look at the effect of trees on house prices. Many researchers have done this, across the world, and the consensus is clear: people are prepared to pay more for houses in neighbourhoods with more trees.

---

* The heatwave of 2003 killed 70,000 people in Europe.

But much of this research raises more questions than it answers. For example, it often fails to distinguish different sorts of trees (e.g. conifers vs. broadleaves), or trees in different places (e.g. garden vs. street trees). Some recent Australian research (in Perth) tried to look at these missing variables. This kind of research is always complicated, for the simple reason that many things influence house prices, and you want to know the *extra* effect of trees, in addition to all these other things. For example, in Perth, all the usual things have big positive effects on house prices, such as more bedrooms or bathrooms, garage space and swimming pools (remember, this is Australia). Like nearly every other study, this one also found a big positive effect on house prices of the presence of trees, in fact AU$16,889 on average. But this effect was found only for street trees; trees actually on a property had no effect, positive or negative, on the price of the house on the same plot.

Given that people generally like trees, this must mean that people also see problems with trees on their own property, such as dropping leaves, damaging paving and drains, costs associated with pruning, thinning and ultimately removal, and possible damage to the house itself (fuelled by paranoid insurance companies). Big trees may also compete for space with other things, such as a veg plot or a patio. In contrast, public trees are seen as providing all the amenity with none of the costs.

There are two messages here for homeowners. First, street trees are valuable things, and you should make every effort to keep them, even if your cash-strapped local authority is reluctant to replace old trees or plant new ones. Losing your street trees could reduce the value of your house by up to 5 per cent. The second message is especially for gardeners: choose the right tree in the first place, plant and look after it properly, and do not be frightened by their (largely imaginary) problems. And don't imagine that starting with a big tree rather than a small one will give you a head start; it won't.

One final thing, which may disappoint those of you who hope that climate change will eventually enable your street to look like Hollywood Boulevard. In the Perth study, house prices were increased only by broadleaved street trees. Palm trees had no effect on house prices.

· · · · · · · · ✳ · · · · · · · ·

Cacti in Britain – outdoors

What are your chances of growing a cactus outdoors in Britain? I mean permanently outdoors, all year round? Slim, I would guess, although hardiness itself is not the problem. I have a *Gymnocalycium* (species unknown), that I filched years ago from the Sierras de Córdoba mountains to the west of

Córdoba, Argentina's second city. The winters there are cold, but very dry, and my specimen has lived in an unheated greenhouse for over a decade, producing several large pink flowers every summer. Clearly it can take the worst our winters can do in terms of temperature, but I suspect if I left it outdoors, our soggy climate would do for it in no time.

Most of northern and western Europe suffers from the same problem, so it's not surprising that a review of cacti in the wild in Europe, published in the journal *Flora* in 2009, reported that the few cacti that have invaded Europe are mostly confined to the Mediterranean. They found not a single record of a cactus in the wild in Belgium, Denmark, Finland, Hungary, Ireland, Luxembourg, Netherlands, Norway, Poland, Slovakia, Slovenia, Sweden or the UK. But, you're thinking, there are a few places missing from that list: Switzerland, Germany and Austria, for example. Indeed, there are a few records from these countries of either *Opuntia humifusa* (eastern prickly pear) or *O. phaeacantha* (tulip prickly pear). The review actually has a photograph of the latter growing on rocks in the Wachau area, near the village of Dürnstein in eastern Austria.

It looks like there are a couple of cacti that don't mind a bit of winter wet, or even snow. So it wasn't really a surprise when that treasure trove of botanical trivia, *BSBI News*, reported *O. phaeacantha* near Maidstone in the summer of 2013. Two plants, clearly enjoying the hot summer, were growing on a steep, sandy, south-facing bank just off the A20, near Junction 8 of the M20. The intrepid botanists were naturally a bit nonplussed by their discovery, whose identity was confirmed by Tony Roberts of the British Cactus and Succulent Society. He also mentioned that not only had he grown it outdoors in Kent for seven years (so right through our recent hard winters), it also flowered and set seed, occasionally giving rise to self-sown seedlings.

So if there are any of you out there who have harboured an ambition to grow cacti outdoors, *O. phaeacantha* looks like the one to try. I should mention it's quite a pretty plant, with showy yellow flowers. Unfortunately the RHS Plant Finder does not list any suppliers, but the *Flora of North America* reports that *O. phaeacantha* and *O. engelmannii* may well be the same thing (they look the same to me), and there is a single supplier of the latter, in Hampshire. On the other hand, there are five suppliers listed for *O. humifusa*, so maybe that's a better bet.

Both *O. humifusa* and *O. phaeacantha* will grow about a foot tall. If you want to try growing them, bear in mind that perfect drainage is the key to success, so plant into a sandy or gravelly mix. Also choose the sunniest possible spot, and however hot and dry the summer, don't water, or use any fertiliser. And wear gloves!

. . . . ❋ . . . .

Eccremocarpus *and the virtues of self-seeders*

A few years ago now, a friend gave me three young plants of *Eccremocarpus scaber*, the Chilean glory flower. Little more than seedlings really. I didn't know much about them, but I carefully selected three spots in my garden and planted them. All three repaid my care and attention by dying, but not before one of them had produced some seeds.

Eccremocarpus seeds aren't particularly small, but they are very flat, and one of them seems to have found its way into a barely visible crack between the house wall and the surrounding concrete apron, where it germinated. It took me a while to realise what this new plant was, and even when I did, I wasn't sure how to react. For those unfamiliar with *Eccremocarpus*, it's a fast-growing climber with finely divided, fern-like foliage and red, orange or yellow tubular flowers. Mine are red. It climbs with tendrils, like a sweet pea, so it needs something to climb up.

Which brings me to an obvious problem. My plant had germinated at the base of a flat wall, and I wasn't about to install a trellis or wires to accommodate it. Nevertheless, I thought I'd let it grow for a while and see what it did. And I'm glad I did, because what happened next surprised me. The tendrils of *Eccremocarpus* are very fine, and although I said the wall is flat, it's not quite smooth. It's rendered with some off-white stuff that gives the wall a rough texture, like extremely coarse sandpaper. Just rough enough, apparently, for my plant to get sufficient grip to support itself.

I watched in amazement as it streaked away up the wall, with no more obvious means of support than those two blokes who climbed El Capitan last winter. By the end of the summer it was about twelve feet tall, and covered in bright red flowers. *Eccremocarpus* is technically evergreen, but survives above ground in only the warmest and most sheltered locations. Mine has disappeared every winter since it first arrived, but is quite happy under the house all winter and always pops up again, twice as vigorous, in the following year.

All of which set me thinking about the virtues of self-seeding garden plants. Would it have ever occurred to me to try to stuff a seed of anything down the aforementioned crack? No it would not, if only because I'd never noticed the crack at all until something started growing out of it. In any case, the Spiderman-like ability of *Eccremocarpus* to grow up a featureless wall wouldn't have occurred to me either. In short, self-seeding has given me a plant I wouldn't have had, in a place I wouldn't have dreamed anything could grow, and all with no effort at all on my behalf.

I know some gardeners look down their noses at self-seeders, but I think we should all be a bit more tolerant. On this subject, as on many others, I don't think I can do better than quote the late, great Christopher Lloyd:

> I never like to weed out anything that I can't identify. Not all seedlings are weeds. You may feel that life is too short to leave a seedling in till it's large enough to identify. My own feeling is that life's too interesting not to leave it there until you can identify it. Taking this view, you will very soon learn to recognise weed seedlings when they are no larger than a pair of seed leaves. The not so easily identified ones will then most probably turn out to be the progeny of some of your border plants or shrubs, and it may suit you to save and grow them on.

I would only add that if it's not noticeably in the way, it might suit you even better just to leave it alone. After all, a self-seeded plant has chosen where it would like to grow, and it's probably a better judge of that than you are.

ON BEING
A GARDENER

Why you should join the BSBI

You may be a member of the Royal Horticultural Society, or of any number of the numerous other societies that cater for gardeners. You are much less likely to be a member of the Botanical Society of the British Isles* (BSBI), and quite possibly you've never heard of it. I know that because the BSBI has fewer than 3,000 members, so there aren't many of you out there. But I'm going to try to convince you that perhaps there should be a few more.

In its own words, 'The BSBI is for everyone who is interested in the flora of Britain and Ireland. From its earliest days it has welcomed both professional and amateur members, and it remains the biggest and most active organisation devoted to the study of botany in the British Isles.' And in case you think 'the flora of Britain and Ireland' has nothing to do with gardeners, BSBI members are as happy talking about introduced plants as they are about natives, and most introductions started out in gardens.

Its professional and amateur mix is reflected in the BSBI's publications. The *New Journal of Botany* is its peer-reviewed, academic journal, and I am not going to try to persuade you to read that. You are not its target audience

* Now the Botanical Society of Britain and Ireland.

and anyway, if it comes to that, I *am* its target audience and even I can't face reading most of it. But the BSBI's other regular publication, *BSBI News*, is quite a different animal, and much, *much* more fun. Nothing botanical is too weird or trivial for inclusion. Let me give you a flavour of some topics aired in recent issues.

Purple toothwort is one of the very few wholly parasitic plants grown in gardens (Roy Lancaster is a fan), and although the books say it parasitises the roots of poplars and willows, there has been much discussion of its many other recorded hosts. The strangest so far is gunnera, which also reveals an odd aspect of toothwort biology: the ground around toothwort-infected patches of gunnera remains soggy even in dry spells. It turns out that like all plants toothwort has to get rid of surplus water, and having no leaves, it does this by simply excreting water into the soil. And in further proof that there's really nothing new, it also turns out that Charles Darwin noticed this too, in 1880.

Given the recent publicity around the urban myth that pampas grass in the front garden advertises the inhabitants' availability for swinging, a short piece by James Armitage (senior botanist at RHS Wisley) caught my eye: 'The sex forms of *Cortaderia selloana*'. Fortunately it's the sex life of the pampas grass itself that is under scrutiny. Pampas grass is dioecious, i.e. it has separate male and female plants, and the flowering plumes look rather different: the female is upright, symmetrical, and generally white. Males are one-sided, slightly drooping, often pink-tinged, and don't last as well as female plumes. Most named cultivars are female, but some are male, and Armitage gives a complete list.

Finally, a longish piece in the latest issue from Simon Harrap, who is writing a guide to wild flowers and wants to ventilate some serious irritation about the inconsistent use of capital letters and hyphens in English names of plants. Indispensable reading if you ever wondered whether to write Marsh Marigold or Marsh-marigold. And believe me, even if you were never puzzled by such a question, you will be after you've read this.

I'm not privy to the editorial policies of *BSBI News*, but an examination of its content suggests something along the lines of 'print everything we are sent, as long as it's not actually libellous or offensive'. In other words it's extremely democratic and inclusive, which is one reason it's such a good read. The downside of such a policy is that botany is no more free of cranks and nutters than any other walk of life, and just occasionally an item appears that is downright bonkers, which – of course – only makes it even more fun to read. In short, *BSBI News* is an insight into a quintes-sentially British (and Irish) organisation, and long may it provide a home for the musings of all those who think plants are just the most marvellous, fascinating things. If you like plants, you have £25 to spare, and you're not a member, I can only ask: why not?

········❋········

Gardeners on Desert Island Discs

Not very many gardeners have appeared on *Desert Island Discs* (*DID*). In fact just eighteen*, compared to, for example, 27 chefs, 72 artists and 68 pianists. Odd when you consider that gardeners are perhaps almost uniquely fitted to actually surviving on a desert island. The first three gardeners to appear are before my time, and the first I can actually remember is Percy Thrower, in March 1963. I don't think I remember Thrower from then (I was only nine in 1963), but he presented *Gardeners' World* from 1969 until 1976, when I certainly do. Wikipedia thinks he might have been Britain's first 'celebrity gardener', although they also think that title might best apply to C.H. Middleton, a well-known broadcaster in the 1930s and 40s. Middleton was in fact the first gardener to appear on *DID*, in November 1943.

---

* I think this is right, but it's hard to be certain. The *DID* archive isn't all that good at listing castaways by occupation. Garden designer Dan Pearson appeared in February 2015, but you'll find him under 'design', not 'gardening'. And he did choose some David Bowie.

Other *Gardeners' World* presenters who have appeared on *DID* include Geoffrey Smith, Alan Titchmarsh and – the most recent gardener to appear, in 2006 – Monty Don. The obvious omission, of course, is the late, great Geoff Hamilton. A black mark for the programme's producers there I think, although to be fair he was probably near the top of their list when he tragically died in 1996.

I should just point out, by the way, that I'm talking here about the names that appear if you search the *DID* website for 'gardeners'. For example, Sir Roy Strong and Germaine Greer do not appear, although both are gardeners, indeed very good ones; they're just chiefly famous for other things.

Other household names to appear are Harry Wheatcroft, Graham Stuart Thomas, Rosemary Verey, Penelope Hobhouse and Christopher Lloyd. Curiously, however, the only other 21st-century gardener guests, apart from Lloyd, Titchmarsh and Don, are not household names at all, or at least not as gardeners. Susana Walton is better known as the wife and later widow of Sir William Walton, although she did create a famous garden. And Anne Scott James is surely better known as a pioneering journalist, although later the author of several classic gardening books.

There's a lesson there for gardeners who would like to be invited onto *DID*: get yourself on the telly, or make sure you're also famous for something else besides gardening.

But what, I hear you ask, about the music? Well, I've said before that no one could really describe gardening as cool, and there's little here to suggest that gardeners are – how can I put this? – down with the kids. There's an awful lot of Mozart, Haydn, Brahms, Bach, Beethoven, Strauss (Johann, not Richard) and Vaughan Williams. Lady Walton showed admirable self-control in choosing only three pieces by Sir William.

If, for the sake of argument, we agree that modern popular music began in 1963 (along with a few other things, according to Philip Larkin), then how much of this has found its way into gardening castaways' choices since then, i.e. from Percy Thrower onwards? Not much – Monty Don turns out to be virtually the sole standard-bearer for pop music, choosing pieces by The Beatles, Bob Dylan, Leonard Cohen, Nick Drake and The Libertines. Otherwise it's a bit of a desert. Rosemary Verey keeps her end up with 'Candle in the Wind' (Elton John's only appearance), and Percy Thrower nearly makes the cut with 'Bobby's Girl' by Susan Maughan (good choice, Percy). But that's it; no David Bowie, no Paul Simon, no Motown, no Kraftwerk (only joking).

Not much evidence, either, that gardeners might have a sense of humour. Dr W.E. Shewell-Cooper, who wrote gardening books from the 1930s to the 1970s and appeared on *DID* in 1965, chose 'Misalliance' by Flanders and Swann. If that doesn't ring any bells, gardening is the clue: it's the one about the 'right-handed honeysuckle and the left-handed bindweed'. But apart from that, nothing: no Tom Lehrer, no Bob Newhart, no Allan Sherman, no Goons (mind you, no George Formby or Benny Hill either, so it could have been worse).

I reckon we're overdue for another gardener on *DID*. Still time to catch up with Beth Chatto.

· · · · · · · ❋ · · · · · · · ·

Gardening and literature

I recently caught up with Mike Leigh's rather splendid film *Happy Go Lucky*. In one scene, the incurably cheerful heroine Poppy, along with her younger sister and best friend, visit her other sister Helen. The visit is not a success; Helen is pregnant and the owner of a husband, a suburban semi, a pension plan and a mortgage, all calculated to alienate her from her free-spirited, single visitors. But just to make sure we get the message, Helen is also in danger of becoming interested in gardening, indicated by her pride in her newly planted roses and busy lizzies.

In my opinion Leigh is being both heavy-handed and lazy here, but in truth he's only following an ancient literary tradition; for centuries, one of the surest ways of signalling to the reader that a character is a bit of a twerp is to make him (usually him) a gardener, and the keener the gardener, the bigger the twerp. I'm sure Jane Austen didn't start this, but she was an enthusiastic promoter of the idea. In *Pride and Prejudice*, Mr Collins, one of literature's great bores and all-round idiots, is of course a keen gardener; in fact it's only his tendency to spend most of his time in the garden that makes him tolerable as a husband for Elizabeth Bennet's old friend Charlotte:

> To work in his garden was one of his most respectable pleasures, and Elizabeth admired the command of coun- tenance with which Charlotte talked of the healthfulness of the exercise, and owned she encouraged it as much as possible.

Another peril of the keen gardener is being bored rigid by their enthusiasm. Again, Mr Collins is typical:

> Here, leading the way through every walk and cross walk, and scarcely allowing them an interval to utter the praises he asked for, every view was pointed out with a minuteness which left beauty entirely behind.

Gardening scarcely features at all in Anthony Powell's mas- terpiece *A Dance to the Music of Time*, but it can hardly be a coincidence that Kenneth Widmerpool – surely a candidate for the most obnoxious individual in 20th-century English fiction – is the only character in the entire twelve-volume sequence with any horticultural connections. Heaven knows Powell gives us plenty of other reasons to dislike Widmerpool, but you know he will come to a bad end when you discover, quite early on, that his father's business was the supply of liquid manure to the gentry. In *The Pursuit of Love*, Nancy Mitford describes with relish the 'boring herbaceous enthusiasms' of Sir Leicester Kroesig, the epitome of herbaceousness, the quintessence of smug dullness. Even some very gifted modern authors have resorted to the motif of the gardener as fool; in Pat Barker's fine *Regeneration* trilogy, we know immediately that one minor medical character is a buffoon, and that his opinions can be ignored, as soon as the poor bloke mentions his roses.

TV's dreadful *Rosemary and Thyme* detective series has rightly been criticised as being hopelessly unrealistic, with two middle-aged ladies tripping over another dead body behind the rose bushes every week, but what did you expect? Rosemary and Laura are gardeners, for heaven's sake, and everyone knows gardening isn't a serious occupation, so we know this is just *Midsomer Murders* with extra horse manure.

How did gardeners come to occupy this peculiar position, somewhere between vicars and traffic wardens? It's all the more surprising when you consider that attitudes to gardening and gardeners in children's literature are generally positive. No one will quickly forget the redemptive power of gardening in Frances Hodgson Burnett's *The Secret Garden*. Several of the books my children loved most when they were small had gardening themes: *The Enormous Turnip*, *Peter Rabbit*, *Jam* by Margaret Mahy (don't tell me you haven't read *Jam*? You'll be telling me next you haven't read *The Great Piratical Rumbustification*), and of course the best of them all, *The Very Hungry Caterpillar*. But it seems that when the time comes to put away childish things, gardening – although far from childish – goes with them.

Lately, gardening has tended to find itself on the unfashionable side in some of society's great debates, including youth vs. age (gardening, like listening to classical music, is something you take up when you're too old for more exciting pastimes, like Glastonbury, snowboarding and riding motorcycles) and class (the gardening classes, whether the owners of flat hats, racing pigeons and whippets, of suburban semis, or of Blandings Castle, have never been the trendy classes). In fact gardening has never been cool; can you picture George Clooney dead-heading his dahlias? No? I didn't think so. Also, despite some mild one-upmanship, gardening is not really a competitive activity, which inevitably makes it a relatively frivolous occupation in the eyes of men, who are generally far more competitive than women.

Returning to the demands of literature, TV and cinema, you also can't get away from the fact that it's hard to make gardening even slightly perilous; 'down these mean streets a man must go' is fair enough, but 'mean allotments' or 'mean herbaceous borders' just doesn't cut it. Indeed, in my experience gardeners are among the most laid-back, generous, serene and above all tolerant people you could hope to meet. In other words, as far as it's possible to get from homicide detectives, terrorists, gangsters and fighter pilots, and certainly not people abounding in possibilities of dramatic tension. So, if the narrative demands a character who's inoffensive and also immediately recognisable as a bit dull, and maybe a bit soft in the head too, gardening is the obvious solution for the lazy author. So, here's a challenge to all you aspiring novelists out there: there's room for a genuinely genre-busting protagonist, a secret agent or private detective who, on his day off, is locked in a life-and-death struggle with vine weevil.

Gardening makes you a better person

Yes, it's true – as I always suspected, gardening *can* make you a better person. And what's more, I can prove it. But you will have to bear with me a bit, since what I'm going to tell you may not, at first, seem to have much to do with gardening. But trust me, it does.

Psychologists have known for a long time that people generally behave more generously and cooperatively than pure self-interest would suggest. A common way of showing this is the so-called dictator game (although to be honest it's hardly a game). One of two players (the dictator) is given a sum of money and asked how he would like to split it with the other player (the receiver). That's it – you see, not much of a game. Simple economic self-interest says the dictator keeps the money, all of it. But in reality shedloads of data show that on average, dictators give around 28 per cent of the money to the receiver. Lots of things determine exactly how much money is given away, but one very important factor is anonymity, or the lack of it. Unsurprisingly, dictators who are being watched, or think they may be being watched, give away more than those who remain anonymous. So powerful is this effect that a simple image of a pair of watching eyes is enough to increase the size of the donation; no real observer is necessary.

Which brings me to some recent research published in the *Proceedings of the Royal Society*. The researchers were looking again at the dictator game, using a large number of players from all over the world, recruited using the online labour market Amazon Mechanical Turk (www.mturk.com; worth a look, incidentally, if you have time on your hands and could use some extra cash). Dictators were, as usual, asked to share (or not) a small sum with an anonymous receiver. One group saw a pair of watching eyes on the screen, while three other groups saw either nothing, a plain black square, or an image of flowers. The expectation was simple: the 'watched' group would donate more, while the others would all give more or less the same.

But the results were surprising. Dictators who saw nothing, or a black square or eyes, did not differ, although they were all rather generous: the most frequent response was simply to split the money 50/50, and on average they gave away 32 per cent. One possible reason for this greater generosity than normal is that academics normally round up undergraduates for this kind of study, and students are notoriously mean (or maybe just notoriously poor). In contrast, most of the participants in this study were not students. But those who saw a picture of flowers gave away significantly more – 38 per cent on average. This result is consistent with other evidence showing a link between viewing nature and a positive emotional state.

For example, patients convalescing from surgery recovered faster and required fewer painkillers if their hospital bed had a natural view, compared to patients with only a brick wall to look at. More generally, viewing natural as opposed to urban scenes can promote feelings of pleasure and enhance attention, and reduce negative emotions such as anger or anxiety. Positive emotional state, in turn, has been linked to increases in sociable and cooperative behaviour. Thus, as the authors conclude, 'we suggest that flower images might have induced positive emotional states in our dictator game players, resulting in the tendency for dictators to donate more to receivers when presented with flower images.'

In other words, looking at flowers (a key aspect of gardening, although of course usually preceded by growing them) increases the stock of human kindness and generosity and thus, I submit, happiness in general. And you can't ask for more than that, can you?

· · · · · · · ·✻· · · · · · · ·

Careers in horticulture

Statistically, I'm on safe ground if I guess you're not a professional gardener. I'm also likely to be right if I assume that a career in horticulture never even crossed your mind when you were younger. According to an RHS survey, almost half of under-25s do not think gardening is a skilled career, and nearly 70 per cent of eighteen-year-olds think gardening should be considered as a career only for those who have failed academically. Basically, gardening is for dropouts, and if a young hoodie finds you weeding a flower bed in your local park, he's likely to assume you're carrying out a community service order; certainly nothing else would induce him to get dirt under his fingernails.

The RHS survey further revealed that 70 per cent of eighteen-year-olds do not think gardening is a career to be proud of, while 79 per cent of those aged 40 or over hold exactly the opposite opinion. Of course there are many young gardeners, but for the most part it seems that gardening, like classical music and crown green bowling, is something that creeps up on people of a certain age. At a time of massive youth unemployment, and with the UK horticultural industry lamenting the growing lack of skilled home-grown job applicants, this is a situation that can only be described as bizarre. Quite apart from the damage to the industry, there's the human cost that comes from (as the survey also found) the 70 per cent of adults who reported that no one mentioned even the possibility of horticulture as a career when they were leaving education.

So, hardly surprisingly, gardening is awash with older career changers who have only just discovered that gardening as a career actually exists. I do just a little bit of teaching on Kew's Horticulture Diploma, and in recent years I've taught (among many others) an ex-policeman, an ex-barrister and an ex-midwife. People who were 30 before they realised they were too charitable to be a police officer, too candid to be a lawyer, and preferred seedlings to babies. It's great that these people, and many like them, have at last discovered gardening, but what a waste that this didn't happen when they were younger. Can't you just feel your heart sink when you read a letter to the RHS magazine *The Garden* lamenting: 'I wish I had been directed towards a career in horticulture instead of a secretarial course.' Ah yes, the secretarial course: the last refuge of the incompetent careers adviser. Emma Thompson's great line (to Carey Mulligan's stroppy teenager) in the film *An Education*, 'It doesn't have to be teaching. There's always the Civil Service', works so well only because it reflects a basic truth about lack of imagination when it comes to careers for school leavers.

Left to themselves, young people all-too-readily associate gardening with the bloke driving a gang-mower endlessly round the local park, or the old chap they see tending his cabbages on the allotment. These are not inspiring images. Instead we need to point to the Olympic Park, the largest new park in London for a century, and a horticultural achievement as stunning in its own way as Danny Boyle's opening ceremony or David Weir's gold medal collection. And to UK horticulture, an industry with a turnover of over £5 billion a year, offering a huge range of careers in retailing, marketing, growing, landscaping, manufacturing, design and logistics. Or maybe we simply need to point out that growing plants is healthy, rewarding and fun, so why would you not want to be paid to do it for a living?

The Royal Horticultural Society and others are doing sterling work in getting gardening into primary schools, but it's later, in secondary school, that teenagers need to be made aware of and enthused about horticulture as a career. Now that the Olympic Park has reopened as the Queen Elizabeth Olympic Park, every school in London should pay a visit. Maybe David Cameron should go too, and discover that horticulture has nothing in common with litter picking.

* * * * * * * * ✳ * * * * * * * *

Status of gardeners

What is a 'gardener'? Most of us are gardeners by default, if only part of the time and sometimes unwillingly. But as long as we can mow the lawn, and we know a dandelion when we see one, we care little that we struggle with some of the finer points of horticulture, and we are happy to call ourselves gardeners, at least some of the time. Which is all very well, but we sometimes extend this haziness about the definition of 'gardener' to those who do it for a living. To cut our hedges, we employ a man who knows even less about gardening than we do, and whose only qualification is knowing where to put the petrol in a hedge trimmer. We pay him the minimum wage, or – in used fivers – a bit less, secure in the knowledge that he probably doesn't deserve much more. Yet we still tell our friends that we employ a gardener and indeed, if asked, that's probably what he would call himself.

But at the same time, most of us are aware that what we admire at Hidcote or Sissinghurst was neither created nor maintained by such people, and that real gardening is a highly skilled job, requiring years of training and experience. That there really are people out there who know how deep to plant a *Cardiocrinum* bulb, or prune *Hydrangea paniculata*, or where it's worth trying to grow *Tropaeolum speciosum* (and more importantly, where it's not). People who could explain the Guyot system for training vines, but who would never be so unkind as to actually attempt to do so. In short, people who could be let loose on our gardens without supervision, in the reasonable expectation that afterwards everything would look a bit better, rather than just a bit shorter.

Unfortunately, perhaps because such people and our man with the hedge trimmer share a job title (but little else), awareness of the crucial distinction doesn't always seem to penetrate very deeply. People do still advertise for a 'skilled gardener', adding that 'experience and horticultural qualifications are a distinct advantage', without recognising the *non sequitur* of then offering £8–10 per hour (wage and quote both from a recent job advert). Worse than that, adverts for gardeners all too frequently add 'general house maintenance and security' or 'occasional driving and general household duties' to the job specification, as though 'gardener' and 'handyman' were virtual synonyms. Or – adding insult to injury – that can't resist adding 'opportunity for the spouse to work on a casual basis in the main house … may include general household work along with some baking and cooking' (again, all quotes from recent job adverts for gardeners).

In case none of this strikes you as odd, try advertising for an 'accountant/handyman' and see where it gets you. Or better still, the next time you visit the doctor, finish up by asking if his wife would like to pop round later and make the beds, before perhaps baking a few scones.

There are bodies that do an excellent job of representing gardeners' interests, for example the Professional Gardeners' Guild, but in the past none with the clout, or perhaps even the ambition, really to safeguard standards and guarantee the qualifications and experience of professional gardeners (most other professions realised long ago how crucial this is). But at last, with the award of a Royal Charter to the Institute of Horticulture, that should have all changed. Claiming not to be able to tell the difference between a real gardener and a man with a van was only ever a pretext not to pay either of them very much, but that excuse is now history. And from there it's a short step to making sure we treat (and pay) real gardeners like the skilled and dedicated professionals they are.